Psalms
For
Ordinary People

by
Sherye Hanson

PublishAmerica
Baltimore

ISBN: 1-4137-0624-X
PUBLISHED BY PUBLISHAMERICA BOOK PUBLISHERS
www.publishamerica.com
Baltimore

Printed in the United States of America

Dedicated to Olivia and Keith
Whose Love is Eternal

About These Poems

When I took a Spirituality Class from Eugene Peterson at Fuller Seminary, he lectured on praying the psalms. I tried to pray them, but I found it very difficult. The psalms were written about problems that seemed to be completely different from mine. One of the most prominent themes of the psalms is enemies. I do have enemies, but they aren't necessary foreign armies or people seeking to kill me. If I wrote poems about my present enemies and about situations with which I could identify, I could pray the psalms more easily.

So I started writing a poem for each psalm for a week. I enjoyed it so much I kept going. Then I shared some with friends and decided to write poems for them all. *The Book of Psalms* is very political. The Psalmists protest against injustice that is done both to themselves, the poor and their nation. Praying these psalms helped me to get out of my own problems and broaden my perspective to the problems of people in other nations and in the poor parts of the world. Poor people, the mentally ill, and the homeless have all sorts of enemies. The poor in the Third World have all the powerful nations of the world against them.

Although Hitler was the most famous maker of holocausts, we had similar things in Uganda, Cambodia, Rwanda, Burundi, Bosnia, Afghanistan, the Kurds, Ethiopia, The Soviet Union, Kosovo, and the Congo. I'm sure I've left out a few. These were more than civil wars – they were outright massacres.

Christians should be protesting these occurrences. We should also complain about the treatment of the homeless and other oppressed peoples. Jesus promised that those who are righteous will suffer persecution – but that is a blessing rather than something to complain about. We need to be complaining about the injustices that happen to others, not just ourselves.

In addition to saying a lot about enemies, the Psalms praise God for His creation, His love, and His power. The psalm writers complain of depression, feel guilty, grateful and angry. All of them are either songs or prayers or both. The audience for the psalms is God. Some of the things that are said are awful. Others are incredibly beautiful.

So why take ancient poetry and tamper with it? I love the shepherd psalm, but except when I was in England, I rarely see sheep. There are many references to ancient Israel and to situations that we no longer think about. In addition, when I put myself into the story, I found it easier to believe that God listens to me and answers my prayers. These are interpretations and are not necessarily accurate. My primary goal is to make it as clear as possible how much God really loves us and that He desires to show mercy more than to give us justice. There will be justice, but before I demand it for myself, I must see that I need mercy, too.

BOOK I

Psalm 1 A Willow and a Tumbleweed

I am a well-watered tree,
A willow growing on the riverbank.
The wind prunes my branches.
The birds build their nests.
The fish rest in my shade.
I'm green all summer long.
Whether in drought or in flood.
I am a well-watered tree.

I was a tumbleweed,
That grew in desert soil.
Any wind would uproot me.
I dried up without rain.

I no longer walk into casinos
I don't stand at the blackjack table,
Nor sit for hours at the bar.

I drink from the spiritual well
That springs up in my heart
I have a story to tell
About the source of health and life.

Psalm 2 For the Twenty-First Century

Why do the nations
Conspire against the poor?
Why does the WTO
Support an unliving wage?

Why do their rulers
Persecute the good?
Why don't they jail
The ones who steal it all?

The Mafia, the drug lords, the slumlords all
Corrupt bureaucrats, democrats and autocrats,
Think they've got away
With their crimes.
They've forgotten the Judgment Day.

You, O God, laugh and say,
"The earth is mine,
There is no God but me."

God will install His Son on Mount Zion
To rule over the earth.
His Son will judge the corrupt and evil.
They will have their day in court.

All will belong to Jesus,
No longer to the rich.
He will engage in mass land reform
And give each one their share.

No longer will the poor
Starve on the land they till.
Instead the harvests will be theirs
To eat their fill.
If you're a king or a president,

Be wise and listen to God,
For soon his Son will rule the earth.
Do what God has said,
"Do justice, love mercy,
And walk humbly with your God."

Otherwise you will be destroyed.
As you tried to destroy the poor.
You will work in sweatshops,
And be hauled off your land.
You will be shot
On the palace steps.

All the refugees,
Fleeing from injustice,
Will find refuge in him.

Psalm 3 For When I'm Afraid of Rejection.
A Psalm of Sherye About Writing

O Lord, I have so many voices
Inside my head that say,
"She's going to fail at writing,
This isn't God's idea but hers."

Every morning I wake up
Eager to write.
When I ask for help
You give it to me.
When I ask for affirmation,
I get a letter from a stranger
Telling me that my writing is an inspiration.

I go to bed and sleep.
I wake up refreshed
Because You have given me peace.
I will not fear the voices
In my head.

Please Lord,
Deliver me from fear.
Let the editors
Read my writing and say yes.

Only You can open their eyes
And open my heart
To pour out
On the page
The love I have for You.

Amen.

Psalm 4 for Sleep

For Britta. With flute. A psalm of Sherye.

Answer me when I call to You.
My God who loves me true,
Relieve me of my depression
And listen to my desperation.

O my excellent God,
Take away the never-ending pain,
And notice the condition that remains the same.

How long, o human, will you prefer others to me?
How long will you love lies to please the Enemy?
Know that the Lord has removed you from the line,
And said to you, "You are mine."

My child, don't get even when you're mad.
When you go to sleep be glad.
For the Lord says, "You are mine."

Praise God and trust Him.

Many ask, "Is there good in all of this?"
Let your light shine through the abyss.
You have filled my heart with delight,
And brought me through the night.

I lie down in the sweet release
Of sleep. In peace,
I dream of You, through the night.

Psalm 5 Protect me from my Enemies
For the Music Director. For flutes. A Psalm of Sherye

There are two kinds of people,
Yours and his
(The good and the bad.)
I'm one of Yours, God.

So listen up.
I've had a rotten day,
I need Your help,
Can You hear me?
Do I need to shout?

Those bad guys –
The ones that murder children
Who lie to their stockholders,
And steal the identities of innocent people
To commit fraud in their name.
You hate them.

So get rid of them.
Find them.
Prosecute them
Show their crimes.
Put them in prison
For the rest of their lives.

Your refugees,
The one who come to you for help.
Protect them from their enemies.
Bring them freedom and justice.
So that they can write music
And sing it.
And not have to worry about war.

Psalm 6 I'm Sorry, God

For the director of music. With guitars. A blues song. A psalm of Sherye

Ah, Lord, don't get mad at me.
Or yell at me for me what I did,
Don't scold me in anger
Or discipline me like a child.
I'm sick and about to pass out.
Lord, heal me. I ache from head to toe.
I feel so guilty for what I've done
How long will it be before You forgive me?

Change Your mind, Lord, and rescue me
Help me, because Your love never stops.
I can't praise You when I'm dead.
I can't remember You when I'm gone.

I'm tired of moaning,
My bed is wet from tears,
My pillow damp from crying.
My eyes are swollen and red
It bothers me that so many hate me.

The Lord has heard me, finally.
He listened to my cry for help
And answered my prayers.
All of my enemies will lose face.
They will suddenly be disgraced.

Psalm 7 For Justice

A blues song concerning a Fugitive. By Sherye.
A Psalm about Justice for the Innocent.

I seek asylum from You.
Protect me from my enemies.
They chase me wherever I go.
If they catch me they'll torture me
And put me in prison.
I'll die with no one knowing what happened.

God if it's my fault
If I'm guilty of a crime
Then the government should arrest me,
Try me and find me guilty.
I should be sentenced and go to prison.

God, You know I'm innocent.
They will not arrest me.
They'll just throw me in jail
Or shoot me in the head.

God, You be the judge
Between them and me.
You know the truth.
Listen to my witnesses.
Examine their evidence.

Then You decide who is right
And who is wrong.
Is the army who imprisons without cause
Or is it an innocent man, who demands justice?

You are my only hope, God.
Only You can see the rightness of my case.
You will wage war against my country.
For killing innocent men, women and children.

You'll send in the Marines.
And arrest the whole gang,
From the dictator who calls himself the president
To privates in the army.

If they don't surrender,
You will invade and conquer them all.
When You come against them.
They won't be able to escape.

They will stumble into the grave
That they dug for us.
They will rot in the prison
They built for us.

Thank You, God, for Your Justice.
I will never stop singing Your praise
Because you rescued me.
Lord God Most High.

Psalm 8 How Do We Rate Your Love?

For the music director. A praise song by Sherye.

O Lord, there is no name on earth
Greater than Yours.
No one is more important than You.
You are vaster than the universe.

Yet You've assigned children and infants
To praise You.
So that Your enemies will hear,
Shut up and listen.

When I look at the sky,
The moon and the stars
That You put into place.
I wonder why You bother with humanity.

What is it about us that makes You care so much about us?
You have given us authority
And we rule over all the earth.
Our status is just a little lower than Yours.

Over farm animals, wild animals,
In the jungle, forest and prairie,
Birds in the sky, fish in the sea,
And all of the other sea creatures.

There is no name higher than Yours, O Lord.

Psalm 9 and 10
An acrostic poem. For the music director by Sherye. Sing with fervor.

Always I will praise You with all of my heart,
Anyone who sees me will hear about Your miracles.
Anywhere I go with You will be my favorite place.
Anytime I see You will be the best time.

Broken are my enemies.
Busted in the act.
Beaten and bruised
Back to their own cave.

Call on the name of the Lord.
Come before his throne.
Cry for help to God.
Claim Your rights from Him.

Delight in Him.
Declare what He has done.
Dare to see victory.
Daily He comes to our aid.

Enemies come
Even the score.
Elevate me so I can
Elevate You

Fallen are the nations –
Feet first into the pit.
Foolish they fought against me,
Fearing neither God nor men.

Gone are my opponents.
Graves are all that's left.
Greatly they have fallen.
Greed strangled their throats.

Hauled off to the pit.
Handed over to death.
Health for the poor
Hope for the hurting.

I want to know You, Lord.
I invite You to answer.
Invisible are You and
Idle when I need You.

Jackals hunt down the weak.
Jump them when they fall down.
Joyful with lust,
Jeer at the Lord and cheer the greedy.

King of kings they ignore.
Kill all thoughts of God.
Kin to the evil one –
King of the thieves is he –

Lords it over the others,
Laps up all the praise,
Lies to cover up his messes,
Loves to curse and threaten;

Menace to society,
Murderer of children,
Mysterious by nature,
Monster in his heart;

Naturally a lion,
Naked in his hunger,
Nothing escapes his eyes.
No one escapes his attack.

Opportunities he waits for.
Open doors he goes through.
Over, above and through he goes
Onto every victim.

Proud of his accomplishment
Prancing before God.
Proven above everyone.
Public in his bravado.

Roust him out, God,
Run him out of town.
Send him down to hell
Save us all from him

Try him,
Test him
Usurp his throne.
Usher in the kingdom

Victory for his
Victims,
Wages for his
Workers·
You alone make him
Yield,
Zealous for the oppressed, the poor, the broken.

Psalm 11 My Hiding Place
For the music director by Sherye

I hide in God,
So how can you say to me,
"Take a getaway car
To your mountain hideaway.
The sheriff is out to get you,
His patrols are stopping every car.
I know that you are innocent –
But the sheriff and the judge are buddies.
Your former boss pays their campaign finances.
With a county as corrupt as ours,
Where else could an innocent man hide?"

God is still in heaven.
He watches every move.
He sees the hearts of the sheriff,
The judge, and his deputies, too.
He knows all about my boss
And the crooked things he has done.
He also knows that there are still
Good people in this county.
He hates the plots of my boss
And the lawmen he's corrupted.

On them will come His justice.
He'll send in the F.B.I.
The I.R.S. will audit every dime.
Long prison terms will be their end.

God is just
And loves justice;
Law abiders will see His face.

Psalm 12 Children and Television

For the Music Director. A Psalm by Sherye

Help us, Lord,
For there is no one
Who does what is right and good.
Help us, Lord.
For there is no one
Who says the things he should.

All men lie
To one another.
They deceive
Our little children
Who crave the things they sell
With their ads of make believe.

Every parent needs
To turn off his TV
Take his children to the park
And watch them play.
Let them run, jump and climb
Until the sky gets dark

"Because the cries of alarm of their parents
For the protection of their children,
I will get up
And protect the children from them."
The Word of God reveals the truth.
His commands their acts condemn.

Lord, keep our children safe
From advertisers and television
They aren't afraid of anyone.
Because advertising is protected

By politicians,
Television stations,
And statisticians.

Psalm 13 Waiting for Healing
For the music director. A Psalm by Sherye

Hey God, I'm still here in Your waiting room,
Did You forget about me?
Why do you hide from me?
My thoughts go in circles as I wait.
Do I have to wait here forever?

Can't You come to me
And tell me to my face
What my prognosis is
And Your treatment plan for me?

Am I going to die of cancer?
Or are You going to heal me?
I want to know.
I'm tired of waiting.

But as I sit here in Your waiting room,
I realize that I trust You completely.
You haven't failed me before.
You always come through for me.

I have a song in my heart
You've been so good to me.
I hate waiting,
But while I do I'll count up all the times
You've saved my life.

Psalm 14 Is Anyone Good Enough?
For the music director. By Sherye.

Is anyone good enough?
The depraved say in their hearts,
"There is no God."
Corrupt and immoral,
They only know evil.

The Lord examines the hearts
Of all the people on earth,
To see if anyone is wise enough
To seek after God.

But no, He doesn't find anyone.
Everyone is out for himself
No one seeks God,
They all want to have their own way,
With no exception.

Will evil people ever learn –
The ones who use people like tissue
Just to be thrown away?
They are totally paranoid –
Afraid of the future.

They know that God sides with those
Who treat everyone with respect.
You corrupt politicians
Take away from the poor
And give to the rich.
Don't you know
That God listens to the complaints
Of single mothers and their children?

How I wish that the Lord would return
To Jerusalem, the holy city.
And restore His Kingdom on earth.
I pray that Israel will be at peace
and Palestine becomes a sovereign nation.
O, that Israeli and Palestinian
Would know the Lord
And love each other.

Psalm 15 Who Lives In God's House?
A Psalm by Sherye

God, who can live with You?
Who rooms in Your house?

The man who lives clean and sober
The woman who gets along with her neighbor,
He tells the truth.
She doesn't gossip.
He does not betray his friends
She doesn't lie about anyone.
He avoids bigots
She chooses friends who honor God.
They keep their promises,
Even when it hurts.
He lends money without interest
She doesn't accuse an innocent person.

No moral earthquake will shake them from their integrity.

Psalm 16 For My Mother
A Psalm of a Vision for my Mother.

God, my hero, I love You.
You are my secret hiding place, my security guard,
And my rescue squad – all in one.

It is to Your hideaway that I escape.

You are my seat belt, burglar alarm, and insurance policy.
I call on You, Lord, who lives up to Your good name.
You come just in time to save me
From depression, fear and loneliness – my worst enemies.

I was about to die,
My lungs were filled with fluid,
My heart had slowed down to forty beats a minute,
I saw death in the face.

With my dying breath,
I whispered, "Lord, help me."
In Your heavenly palace,
You heard my whisper,
While the party was going on,
You listened to my call.

Then, with a voice of thunder,
Lightning struck beneath Your feet,
From a dark tornado cloud,
You came.
You pushed death out of the room,
Sucked the fluid from my lungs,
And touched my heart and it was strong again.
I got out of bed, alive and whole,
Ready to go back to work.

SHERYE HANSON

While You were in my hospital room,
War of the worlds raged outside.
Death and all his allies
Staged a nuclear war.
Buildings fell.
Cities burned.
Mushroom clouds filled the sky.
Whole populations turned into shadows on walls.
The world burned.

In the middle of this, in my hospital room,
You were breathing life to life into my mouth,
And massaging my heart.
You brought me back to life.

When I stood up shakily,
You took my hand.
We saw the battle from the safety
Of my hospital tower.
Blasts crushed the buildings below us.
Bombers buzzed the sky.
Fire trucks hooted horns,
And blew sirens.
Smoke poured out of burning buildings.
People ran down streets full of flame.
Tears ran down my face,
"For this You saved me?"
Then in an instant,
Like changing a channel,
The scene changed.
The city was full of activity,
Traffic jams, shoppers walking,
And children getting off of buses.
A homeless woman with three large shopping bags
Stumbled to a park bench.
All was as usual again.

He said to me,
"I wanted you to see the other side,
Where all the battles are fought.

Death didn't want me to come here,
He was almost finished with his job,
But when I came out of heaven,
I encountered the enemy,
He should have known
He has no super bomb
That can put an end to me.
For I have defeated death,
And risen far above it."

I glanced down at His hands,
When He saw me looking,
He lifted them up
And opened His hands, palms up.
I saw the scars,
I knew it was He,
Though He dressed like
A nurse or doctor in scrubs,
With a stethoscope around His neck.

He gave me a big hug
And helped me to get dressed,
He signed me out,
Put me in a wheelchair
And wheeled me out to the street.
Where my family and friends were waiting.
They had rented a limousine,
For a party instead of my funeral.
They took me to the top
Of the Seattle Space Needle.
They'd rented out a room.
We celebrated my grand recovery.

We talked about how God had saved me.
They told me how they had gotten the call.
The hospital staff mentioned miracles.
My doctor said, "I've never seen anything like it,
An old woman whose heart was made new,
Who a moment before was dying.
They said that the Lord told them,

31

He saved my life for a purpose,
He still needed my services.
I was one of His favorites.

I needed to spend my time,
In reading the scripture
And prayer.
The health and influence
Of my granddaughters
Was on the line.
If I read, meditated and prayed.
I could bring them through the storm
Of mental illness and despair.
They would grow to be
Mighty women of God.
They would reach those
Everyone else ignored.

Kristina would explain the Bible
To people who couldn't understand it.
She would teach them to live it
And train them to be disciples,
Who would carry the message to the world.

Britta would talk to everyone,
The quiet one would open her mouth.
Telling strangers about God,
Bringing foreigners to Jesus,
And presenting them at church.

This is what God had told them
In their conversation.
He had healed me for a purpose.
To provide spiritual support,
An oasis on the journey
Of school, career and marriage.

He had plans for me.
And wanted me to stick around.

As they told me their stories,
We toasted and cheered,
Laughed and cried,
And celebrated until midnight.
Tears ran down my cheeks.
Laughter split my sides.
I went home tired and happy.
To my new home.
I fell asleep,
The minute my head
Hit the pillow.

Psalm 17 I'm Innocent
Prayer of an Innocent Man. A Psalm by Sherye

God, listen to me,
Don't turn away.

I'm not lying
So please pay attention.
Tell everyone that I'm innocent
And didn't commit the crime.

You can check out my story.
And verify the facts.
You can question me for hours
But you'll find that I haven't
Done anything wrong.
I've decided that I will not lie.

As for what other people do,
I keep my mouth shut.
I don't pay any attention
To the violent.
I keep to your way.
I haven't slipped up.

I call to You for help, Lord, because I know You'll answer,
So answer me.
Show me how much You care,
Save me.
Rescue me from my enemies.
Keep special watch over me
As Your favorite child.
Hide me under Your skirt
From the bullies
Who are all around.

They don't care what they do
Just brag about how
They will hurt me
When they catch me.
They know where I am.
And watch for the chance
To catch me off guard.
They are like a lion ready to pounce.

Stand up, Lord, get them
Before they get me.
Their pay is on earth.
You quiet the hunger of Your children
Their children are full
They have money to give to their kids,
My only reward is waking up
To see Your face.

Psalm 18 God My Hero

To Brian, who has been Clean for Ten Years

I love you Lord, my hero.

You are my rock of Gibraltar, my castle, my knight.
My God is a mountain of iron,
I can hide on You.
You are my defense and alarm.
I can always call on You; You are dependable.
No enemy can hurt me when You are here.

I was caught in a trap and couldn't get loose,
The floodwater rose up to my throat.
I was just about to drown.
Panicked, I held out my hands for You.
You saw me and rescued me.
Even when I couldn't shout, You heard me.
The fault slipped and the ground trembled,
Solid earth wavered like the waves of the ocean,
The mountain erupted and smoke poured out,
Lava spilled over its sides.
Fire rose into the sky.
Hot rocks spewed from the crater.

Then the Lord pushed away the smoke.
He got into His starship and flew
On the layers of air.
The dark clouds hid Him,
He burst out of the clouds
Through missiles and bombs,
Which exploded and crashed to the ground.
The enemy ran for their lives.
Seas parted,
Tsunamis flooded the beach.
Bombs left deep craters.

I heard Your voice over the noise.
The blast of Your breath
Gave heat to my body.
You picked me up
And carried me.
My enemies looked but couldn't find me.
You took me out of hell
And brought me into heaven.

You did this because I trusted in You
And did what You asked me to do.
I turned away from my old ways
And listened to Your words.
I followed them all.
And kept clean.

To those who trust You, You are trustworthy
To those who do right, You do right.
To the genuine, You are genuine.
Yet, to the corrupt You are wise.
You save the ordinary,
But humiliate the arrogant.

Lord, don't let my candle go out.
Guide me through the unknown.

With Your help I can go against an army
I can climb up any wall.

God, Your map is accurate,
Without mistake.

You protect
All who hide in You.
Who else is there but You?
What mountain is there but our God?
He's the one who energizes me
And maps out my path
With certitude.

I'll never get lost with His compass.

I can climb slippery mountains
With His shoes on,
They cling on the steepest path.

He teaches me rock climbing.
I know how to hammer in each piton
Pick the safest hold
And tie the perfect knot.
My rope is the strongest nylon.
The master climber trained me.
I will not fall and twist my ankle.

No gravel will make me slip.
Ice will not resist my crampons.
No cliff is too steep or too sheer.
The wind is not strong
Enough to knock me down.
No mountain can defeat me.
I've climbed them all.
My oxygen mask never slips.
And my tank never runs out of air.
You've taught me every thing
I need to know about this mountain.

Blizzards will not cover me.
I shake off all the snow.
Each step I take is sure.
I'll reach the top.
Others fall around me,
Run out of air.
Drop their axes.
And lose their gear.
They die of thirst
And starve to death.

Psalm 19 My Instruction Manual
For the music director. A Psalm by Sherye

God's signature is on the skies,
He painted them so blue,
Every day they change, showing His handiwork.
Every night, the stars that shine
Against the midnight sky
Tell everyone who sees
About Your love and wisdom.
They speak as loudly in Kenya
As they do in Australia.
No hamlet or city cannot hear their voice.

In the sky He has placed a canopy for the sun,
Under which the wedding of sun and sky
Can celebrate.
The sun is like a runner who after he's run the race,
Runs in front of his fans, with his hands raised high.
It makes a circuit from the east to the west.
Nothing can hide from its heat.

Just as the natural laws are perfect,
So are the laws of the Lord.
They bring the soul back to life.
He wrote statutes, precepts and commands
And gave them to Moses,
Who passed them on to us.

These laws can make us happy if we obey them,
And sad if we disobey them.
God wrote us an instruction manual
For how to live a joyful, constructive life.
He gave these eternal principles
To us because He loves us.
Gold is precious, but His laws are more so.
Honey is sweet, but His principles taste better.

They warn against stupidity and
Lead us into a good life.

Does He make mistakes?
No, but I do.
Lord, forgive those faults
That no one sees but You –
The 'I want to do it my way' sins.
I want You to rule over me
I don't want sin to reign in me.

I want both what is in my heart
And comes out of my mouth
To please You.
O my wonderful God.

Psalm 20 A Blessing For The Costa Rican President
Whose Country Does Not Have a Military.
For the music director. A Psalm by Sherye

May the Lord save you when you are in trouble,
His name protect you from your enemies.
And His angels watch over you.

May He remember what you've given up for Him,
And accept your sacrifice of praise.

May He give to you,
That for which you secretly wish
And make your plans succeed.
We will cheer for you when you win
And give you a party to celebrate.
May God give you all for which you ask.

I know that God listens to Jesus,
He sits at God's right hand,
Some trust in tanks and others in fighters,
But we trust in the name of the Lord.
They are humiliated and crushed
But we stand tall.

O Lord, save our nation.
Answer us when we pray.

Psalm 21 For George W. Bush

For the music director. A Psalm by Sherye.

O Lord, the president admires Your strength,
He gives You the credit when we win.
You have given him the desire of his heart –
To be the president.
You have welcomed him with the blessings
Of many church leaders,
And made him the most powerful man in the world.
He asked for many days in office
And protection for his life.
So far You have given to him
All for which what he asked.
Through the victories You gave him in Afghanistan
His glory is great.
You gave him the admiration of many.
Certainly You granted him eternal blessings
And he enjoys being in Your presence.
He is a Christian who trusts in the Lord,
And Your unfailing love will protect his life.

Your hand will capture
Bin Laden and Saddam Hussein.
And when You appear,
You will make their lives miserable.
You will swallow them up
And Your anger will consume them.
You will destroy their children
And they will have no descendants.
Though they plot against America
And blow up a resort in Bali,
They will eventually fail.
For You will shame them
When You capture them.

We praise Your strength
And sing about Your power, O Lord.

Psalm 22 When I Quit the Pastorate

For the music director. A blues song. A Psalm by Sherye.

My Lord, My Lord, why have You left me?
Why did You desert me
In my time of greatest need?
I call Your telephone number twenty times a day,
But You do not answer.
I call in the middle of the night –
But I hear nothing.

Yet You are God,
The Jesus we worship,
Our ancestors trusted in You
And You rescued them from Sweden
They cried to You
And You brought them
To America, where they could worship You
With a pure conscience.

Look at me! I'm not a woman.
I'm a big fat zero.
I am looked down on by the superintendent
And despised by the M.E.G. board.
All the former pastors who see me
Act as if I'm not there.
They shake their heads
And think,
What did God see in her.
She thinks God will save her reputation.
Let her try – she thinks God is on her side.

Yet God, You were with the doctor
When he delivered me at birth.
Even when I drank my first bottle,
You were there.
You have always been my God,

From conception until now.
Don't leave me alone
For I'm in trouble.
I don't have anyone else.
Many church leaders surround me,
The ones who have influence have written me off.
I am a nobody in their circle.
They gossip about me.

I am completely drained.
My joints hurt.
My strength is gone,
My mouth is dry.
I feel sick enough to die.
Gossips surround me,
Those who hate me
Are the ones who
Make all the decisions.

God, come near,
Strengthen me with Your Strength,
Deliver me
From persecution.
My ministry
From liars and gossips.
I will tell all my friends
About how wonderful You are.
Those in my house and my church,
Will praise You.
You, who love God, praise Him.
All of you, descendants of immigrants,
Honor Him.
For He hasn't despised or rejected
My suffering.
He has not hidden His face from me
But He picked up the telephone
And came to my rescue.

From You, Lord, comes
The core of my sermon.

Before those who love You
I will fulfill my call.
The poor will eat and have enough.
Those who seek God
Will praise Him.
All the people of the earth will honor Him.
For Power belongs to the Lord.
He rules over the earth.

All the rich and powerful
Will eat at his table,
Those buried in graves
Will rise up, worship Him.
All generations will worship God.
They will tell how good He is
To those who are not yet born
For He took care of me.

Psalm 23
A Psalm by Sherye

The Lord is my pastor
I lack for nothing.
He refreshes my soul with wonderful sermons.
The hymns He chooses, speak directly to my heart.
I leave the sanctuary revived and ready for the rest of the week.

He challenges me to walk in the spirit
In the middle of the secular world

Which is full of spiritual and physical danger.
His words discipline me to follow Him.
His prayers comfort me.

He meets with me at the coffee shop downtown,
Where He buys me scones and coffee
And discusses all the challenges I face.
He praises me for the decisions I make.

He prays with me and hugs me
As we leave the coffee shop.
His love and kind words follow me
Where ever I go.
Everyday is Sunday
When I'm with Him.
Someday I will live with Him in His house
And enjoy His love and kindness forever.

Psalm 24 The Earth Belongs to God
By Sherye. A Psalm

The earth belongs to God,
And all that is upon it.
For He raised up the land out of the sea.
And lifted it above the waters.

Who can come up the Lord's hill?
Who can stand in His holy presence?
The one who is innocent of violence
And whose heart is pure.
He doesn't worship money
Or swear to tell lies.
He will receive gifts from God
And will be found innocent
By Jesus, His advocate.
This is what happens
To those who look for Him,
Who want to know You personally,
O God of all the earth.

Lift up your gates,
Gates,
Open up your ancient doors,
That the Glorious King
May enter your city.
Who is the Glorious King?
Our powerful God
The one who wins
All spiritual battles.

Lift up your gates,
Gates,
Open your ancient doors
That the Glorious King
May come in.

Who is this Glorious King?
Our powerful God
He is the Glorious King.
Hurrah!

Psalm 25 Teach Me, God
By Sherye. An Acrostic.

Always I open my heart.
Before Your face,
Care for me.
Don't let my enemies
Elevate themselves over me.
Free me from their grasp.
Give me peace
Hope and love.
Invite me to Your classroom,
Jealously protect my place
Keep me on the right path,
Listen to my needs.
Meet me on the road.
Never leave me.
Open my eyes to see Your mercy and love.
Past sins and rebellion tripped me up
Quickly You saved me from them.
Remember me according to Your love.
Stately and honorable is the Lord,
Under His guidance we will never fail.
Victory is for those who listen to You.
Whoever fears the Lord is teachable.
Expect great things from God.
You will lead us to wisdom, wealth and peace.
Zion is Your holy hill – Redeem Your people, Lord

Psalm 26 I'm Innocent
By Sherye

Clear my name, Lord,
For I am innocent.
I have always trusted You
Completely.

Check me out – body, mind and heart.
See that I love You and think upon You.
Like a brand-new lover with her love.
I don't surround myself with liars,
I don't spend my time with hypocrites.
I hate being with phonies
And refuse to sit with the pretentious.
I wash my hands before I go to confession.
I praise You loud and long.
I brag about Your miracles
To whoever will listen.
I love to go to church.
To worship your name.

Protect me from thieves and murderers.
Who plan out their crimes.
They bribe as many police officers
And judges who will accept their bribes.
But I'm not like that
I am pure and holy.

You look at me and say, "You were just like
All humanity – a sinner."

I have to admit that I was.
But now I'm a sinner with a difference –
I've been saved from sin and guilt.
I'm walking on a new path.
My feet are on solid ground.

Psalm 27 God in the City
By Sherye

The Lord is my guide and my Savior.
Is there anyone I should fear?
The Lord is my steel door
Who can go against Him?
When rapists try to hurt me.
To bring me shame,
When muggers hit me over the head,
They will be caught.
Though an entire gang attack me,
I won't be afraid,
If a drive-by shooting happens on my street,
Even then I will be secure.

One thing I ask of God,
This is what I want,
To live in God's house
For the rest of my life.
To look into His face,
And listen to His voice.
For when trouble comes,
I will be safe in His house.
He will hide me.
In the shelter of his arms.
Then I will walk down the runway
In front of all my enemies.
I will dance on stage before the Lord.
I'll sing, shout and play in the band.
All for You.

Listen to me,
God.
Please answer me.
My heart says,
"Turn to the Lord."

I look for You.
Don't turn Your back on me.
Don't turn away in anger.
You've been my best friend,
Don't leave me now.
O God my Savior.
Though my parents gave me up
For adoption.
I've found a home in You.
Give me Your lessons.
Lead me in the right direction
Away from those who would hurt me.
Don't turn me in to the police;
They won't believe me.
They'll listen to the defense attorney
Of the rapist,
Who will line up witnesses
To destroy my reputation.

I have this hope
That I will see God's goodness
While I'm still alive.

Wait for God.
Be Strong.
Don't worry.
Just wait for God.

He'll come.

Psalm 28 A Call for Help
By Sherye

I call You, Lord, my foundation.
Don't pretend to be deaf with me.
For if You keep quiet,
I will be like the miners
Who go into the pit
Never to return.

Hear my call for help
I'm dialing 911.
As I lift my face
Towards heaven.

Don't let them pick me up in a paddy wagon
With murderers and thieves.
The ones who say hello and smile
But curse you when You're gone.
Prosecute them, Lord,
Judge them and find them guilty,
Send them to jail and make them pay.
That is what they deserve.
They don't care about You, God,
And all You've done for them.
You must lock them up
For a long, long time.

Praise be to the Lord,
For He has heard me.
The Lord is my attorney
My advocate in court,
I trust Him completely
For He has represented me well.
I am very happy,
I will sing to Him a song.

The Lord defends His people,
He protects His president,
Save our nation and bless it
Be our shepherd and carry us forever.

Psalm 29 His Power

A Psalm by Sherye

Praise the Lord, you people with power,
Honor Him for His glorious strength.
Give to the Lord the glory He deserves.
Worship our holy and beautiful Lord.

We hear God's voice above the water,
Our glorious God thunders
Louder than the mighty Columbia,
He roars like tumbling water
Thunders and booms,
He splits the mighty fir trees
Of the Olympic Mountains.
Mount Rainier leaps like a dancer,
Mount Baker skips like a young girl
God strikes like lightning,
And shakes the Valley.
His voice carries from Everett to Olympia
His thunder twists the fir trees,
And fells them into piles,
Together His people shout,
"Glory, glory, glory."

Mightier than all the rivers
Of the Puget Sound,
God sits on His throne forever.
He both strengthens His people for battle
And blesses His people with peace.

Psalm 30 Of Gratitude
A Psalm for dedication of the church
That I never was able to build.

I will honor You, o Lord,
For You lifted me out of dishonor.
My enemies were happy
To see me fall down,
I called to You for help
And You lifted me up.
You brought me from death to life.
And spared me from the grave.

Sing to God, those He has saved.
Praise His holy name.
He gets angry only for seconds,
But He loves us over our lifetime.
We may cry for a night,
But we rejoice
At morning light.

When I felt safe, I said,
"Nothing will bother me."
God, when You loved me,
You made my house secure.
But then You disappeared
And I was afraid.

I called, "Help me."
What good is it if I die?
Can a corpse praise You?
Will my dead body
Say good things about You?
"Please, listen and save me."

You turned my tears to joy,
When You exchanged

My hospital gown for a ball gown.
That I might dance all night
And sing Your praises at midnight.
Thank You. Thank You. Thank You.
Amen.

Psalm 31 My Help
For the Music Director. A Psalm by Sherye

I'm hiding out in You.
Please protect me.
Deliver me.
Listen to me
And hurry please.
Be my safety net
And my life jacket.
You are my security locks
And burglar alarm.
My reputation depends on Your help.
Lead and guide me – out of the trap
That has been set for me,
Once I leave this house.
I put my very life into Your hands,
Save me, One True God.

I hate those worthless idols –
Money, power and fame.
I trust in God instead.
I love You and enjoy Your love.
For You saw my problem
And solved it.
You didn't give me away
To the enemy
But You put me into a safe place.

"Help me, Lord, for I am in trouble.
My eyes hurt from crying.
I cannot see
Mourning weakens my heart and soul.
The cancer grows,
Slowly but every day
I am weaker.
My bones break from brittleness.

My neighbors shut their doors to me.
My friends refuse to visit.
Whoever sees me on the street
Avoids me and walks on the other side.

No one remembers me.
I could be dead for all they care –
A broken pottery jar,
Reduced to shards,
Slander, plots and conspiracy –
I hear new ones every day.
I turn off the radio
And the television.
I can't listen anymore.

Instead, I trust in the Lord,
I tell everyone I see,
"The Lord is my God."
You determine how long I will live.
Save me from my enemies,
From those who pursue me.

Send me Your bright smile
So that I know that You still love me.
Don't let me be embarrassed
Because I called on You.
Shame the enemy
By catching him in his lies.
The enemy accuses the honest
Of what he does himself.

Such a generous God You are.
You store a closet full of presents
For those who love You.
You give them to Your friends
On stage in front of everyone.
You hide Your friends from those
Who would harm them.
In Your house they are safe
From the accuser.

Praise the Lord,
Everyone,
For the way He shows His love.
When enemies
Surrounded the city,
You heard me
In spite of all the noise
And confusion.
When I called to You
For Help
You came quickly
And defeated the enemy.

Love the Lord
All His children
He will take care of You.
Be strong,
Be courageous
All who hope in the Lord.

Psalm 32 My Sins are Forgiven.

By Sherye. A Hymn of Praise

Happy is the man whose sins God forgives,
Happy is the woman when God does not count her sins
After she admitted them to God.

When I pretended everything was all right
My bones dissolved
And I was in constant pain.
I felt guilty day and night.
I had no energy
I faded like a flower in the summer's heat.

Then I admitted that I was wrong.
I no longer hid my sins.
And said, "I did it, God,
I lied, cheated and stole."
Then You said to me,
"I forgive you."

So I suggest that you be honest.
Pray and ask forgiveness
As soon as you can.
When you die,
It will be too late.

You are my secret passageway.
Through You I escape danger.
You surround me with triumphant songs.

As your teacher, I will instruct you.
As your counselor I will give you the best advice.
Don't be like a horse,
That has to be controlled by a bit and bridle,
Who will not follow without them.
Those who disobey have many problems.

But the Lord's never-ending love
Provides a warm nest for those
Who trust in Him.
They are happy, joyous and free.
Sing out,
You, who trust in God.

Psalm 33 He is Our God

Sing with enthusiasm, God's children.
His people should always praise Him.
Praise Him with the piano,
Make music on the twelve-string guitar.
Write for Him a new song,
Perform it well and sing it loud.

For God's words are honest and good.
We can always depend on Him.
The Lord loves whatever is good and just,
He fills the earth with His eternal love.

He spoke and the heavens appeared
Entire constellations lit up by His breath.
He fills up the aquifers with water
And places the deep waters in storage.
Let everyone respect the Lord,
Let them be afraid of His power,
For He spoke
And wow,
The universe lit up.
He said to the land, "Dry out,"
And it hardened.

Nations plan wars
But God interferes.
God schedules events
And keeps to His appointments
For every generation.

What a happy nation
That has "I Am" as its God.
He chose them as His inheritance.
God sees all humanity,

He forms all of our hearts,
And evaluates what we do.

The size of His army
Never saves a president.
No soldier escapes
By his wits alone.
No Hummer can save you.
Despite how well it's made.
God watches those who trust Him.
Those who hope only in God
To deliver them from war
And famine.

We wait with expectation
For God's help and protection.
We get excited when we hear His name.
Love us forever, O Lord
For all our hope is in You.

Psalm 34 God is Good.
By Sherye When He rescued me.

Forever I will praise the Lord.
I will describe for you his attributes.
I will consider
Every aspect of his character.
If you are in trouble,
I have something to say to you.
Today you will hear
The story of how God saved me.

I looked for God but He found me.
He took away all my fears.
After I look into his face,
My face reflects His light
As the moon to the sun.
No longer do I hide my face in shame.
This poor woman called,
And the Lord heard me,
He rescued me from a police raid.
The Lord's angels surrounded our house
And He delivered all who live here.

Smell, taste, hear, touch and see –
Isn't the Lord good?
Respect the Lord, you who serve Him,
For those who trust Him will need nothing.
Corporate executives may become weak and hungry.
But those who run after God will have
Everything they need.

Children, come to me.
Sit on my lap
So I can tell you bedtime stories.
I will teach you all about God.
If you want to live a long life,

Then tell the truth in love.
Turn from evil and do what's right.
Seek peace with your neighbors.

God's eyes watch out for those who obey Him.
His ears listen for their cries for help.
God's face turns away from those who disobey.
His hands remain in His lap.

The obedient cry out and God listens,
He saves them from what they fear.
The Lord loves the brokenhearted
And saves those with no self-esteem.

Psalm 35 Drug Addicts Need God, Too.

By Sherye.

Methamphetamine is the drug
That seduces my friends
Contained in a tiny plastic bag,
It gives them a powerful high.
Be to my friends
A desire stronger than drugs.
Save them from their craving.
Fill them with pure love.

Why is it that when you're down,
Everyone has to tell you – I told you so.
Why did you try this crazy plan?
If you invite drug users in your house,
They will take advantage of you.
To your face they will tell you,
That they want to change.
Behind your back,
They take you for a fool.

I have prayed night and day for them,
That they would lose their desire for drugs.
That they would surrender to You
And do Your will instead of their own.
But they didn't listen to You or me.
They did something they knew was wrong.

We had no choice to report our stolen car.
Not really knowing
Whether our friends had taken it.
Now they are in jail.
The cops had to arrest them.
The police think we are stupid,
Our son thinks we enable them.

All I know is that I have a broken heart.
They have broken my trust.

We could not protect them
From their own offense.
The officer waited until they came home
And arrested them in our driveway.
He cuffed them and searched them
And found drugs they said they didn't use.
I was only sad,
Sad that they broke our trust,
Sad that once more they would go
Through the system again.

O Lord, all I want is for them
To know You
And the power of Your love.
To replace a craving for drugs.
With a desire to know You.
Be with them in jail.
Wear the red pajamas.
Sit by their side.

They called and told Scot's girlfriend
That they had taken my car.
They would return in an hour.
Meanwhile we went to church.
We prayed on the way.
Give us wisdom and strength.
To do what is right.

We went into the garage,
They sat ashamed, afraid.
They lied to us
And cried to us.
We forgave
And welcomed them home.

But I had to call up the police.
Who weren't too happy with me.

My car had returned and so had they.
I told him their names.
Knowing full well that their history
Soon would be known.

Comfort and instruct them.
May all those who told us so
Not worry about us,
But pray for our addict friends
That God would
Turn their hearts from drugs
And focus on You.

Psalm 36 A Sermon Against Sin
For the Music Director. A Psalm by Sherye, one of God's servants.

The Lord has put in my heart,
A sermon against sin.
Sinners do not respect God.
They are so arrogant
That they can't see what they've done wrong.
They lie to others and deceive themselves.
Once they were wise,
And did what was right.
Now, even in bed, they plan evil.
The sinner has committed himself
To the inevitable path of destruction.

Your love reaches higher than Mount Everest
Lord, Your justice to the deep canyons in the ocean.
You provide for both human and animal.
There is no price tag for Your eternal love.
Both presidents and single mothers
Find safety in Your presence.
They both eat well at Your Thanksgiving Table.
You hand them a goblet of living water,
Their faces glow from the candelabra of Your love.

Don't stop loving me, o God.
I know You and desire to serve You
With all of my heart, mind and body.
Protect me from those who would harm me.
See how the sinners lie in drunken sleep.
But for Your grace I'd be down there, too.
Wallowing in self-pity and anger.
A good woman still has problems,
But God solves them all.
He protects a good man's bones.
None of them will break.

Evil devours those who do evil.
God condemns the enemies
Of those who wait His tables.
God doesn't punish
Those who repent
And turn to Him.

Psalm 37 Ordinary People
By Sherye

Don't worry about the bad guys
Or envy those who disobey the law.
For they are just seasonal
They die from a hard frost.

Depend on God and do what's right,
Live off the land and enjoy its fruits,
Delight in God
And He will give you
Your innermost desires.

Make a commitment
To do things God's way.
Trust that He will keep His promises.
He will make the good actions you do
Shine in the morning
And your case will be judged as true
As the noonday sun is bright.

God's waiting room is full
Don't worry, He hasn't forgotten.
Don't worry about those who cut into the line,
And try to get there first.

Don't get mad or get even,
That only gets you in trouble.
Evil men and women
Will be written out of His will.
But those who hope in God
Will inherit the earth.

In just a few years,
There will no longer
Be evil people.

You'll try to find out where they went.
They will have disappeared.
But those ordinary people
That no one thought much about,
They will take over the land
And live in peace.
The rich evil landlords,
Try to destroy those who protest
Their oppression,
But God makes sure that good people,
Who till the soil,
Will once again inherit the land.

The army goes out
With machine guns and tanks
To destroy the poor.
God sees and hears
And soon He'll send His own army
And the soldiers will die
By their own bullets.

It is better to live in
The hut of a good man,
Than the mansion of a drug lord.
For the power of the drug lords
And landlords will be broken.

God knows how long
The blameless will live.
Their inheritance is forever.
When drought comes they won't wither.
When famine results they will eat well.

But the landlords will die off.
God's enemies will be burned up
And vanish like smoke.

The wicked borrow money but don't pay back.
Good people give generously
To those who can never repay.

Happy are those to whom
God gives the land.

Those whom God cuts off will be ashamed.
The Lord frequently cuts back the branches
That block the road.
He opens the way,
So that all can follow Him.
If I trip, I will not fall,
For the Lord holds my hand.

I was young once, can you believe it?
Now I am old as you can see.
Yet in all my years I've never seen
God abandon His people
And allow their children to have nothing to eat.
He rewards their generosity
By keeping for their children bread on the table.

Turn away from evil and do what is right.
Then you will live on your land forever.
For the Lord takes care of those who obey Him
And doesn't abandon those who keep their word.

God will always protect the dependable.
But the children of the wicked will suffer.
Those who obey Him will inherit the land
And live in it forever.

Good men speak wisely.
They show common sense,
God's law is in their hearts.
Their feet do not slip.

Evil men surround good men,
To murder them and take all they have.
God will take good men
Out of their power
Nor will He let them be condemned
If brought to trial.

The Lord's waiting room is full.
But don't despair.
He will take care of you
And return to you your land.

Psalm 38 Forgive Me, Lord
A Psalm of Sherye. A Request.

O God, please don't scold me
Or discipline me.
I know You are angry with me.
I feel guilty
I know what I've done wrong.
The Holy Spirit told me that I'd tripped up.
I feel despair to my bones.
My guilt overwhelms me
It is too heavy for me to carry.

My broken heart won't heal.
It is like an infected wound.
I am totally humiliated because of my sin.
I'm heartbroken with guilt,
My back hurts,
I'm sick all over.
I am weak and completely crushed.
I feel absolutely terrible, God.

You know what I long for, God,
You can hear my sighs.
My heart beats too fast,
I am too weak to stand.
Even the brightness of my eyes is dulled.
My friends and family ignore me.
My neighbors avoid me.
My enemies want to get me
Now that I am down.

I cannot hear,
I cannot talk.
I have nothing to say.
I wait for You, My God.
You will answer me, My God and Savior.

I asked of You,
"Don't let my enemies
Treat me with disrespect.
They are happy when I stumble."

I am falling.
My pain never goes away.
I feel guilty about my sin.
All I want is to repent of it and forget it.
I have many powerful enemies.
The list grows longer every day.
They repay my help with harm
And lie about me when I'm doing what's right.

Lord, don't give up on me.
Stay close, o God.
Come as fast as You can to rescue me.
My Lord and Savior – Jesus Christ.

Psalm 39 A Momentary Life

For the Director of Music. A Psalm of Sherye.

I told every one, "I will be quiet
And not complain
As long as the ones who harmed me
Are sitting right next to me."
Keeping it to myself
Just made me feel worse.
My anger grew,
The more I thought
About what had happened
To me.

Then I asked God,
"Tell me how my life is going to be.
Am I going to live past sixty?"
Even ninety isn't very long
Compared to an eternity.
My life is just a moment.
Human beings are like ghosts
We busy ourselves with things
That will disappear as soon
As we're gone.
We save money, but don't know
Who will get it.

So God, what should I expect?
All I hope for is in You.
Save me from my sins,
And the scorn of the gossips.
I was the quiet one, who never said a word.
This is the way You made me.
Take away Your hand
That keeps me from speaking out.

Listen to me.
Help me.
Don't ignore my weeping.
For I am like a stranger to You.
Don't look at me – I want to be happy
Before my life is over and gone.

Psalm 40 For a Sweatshop Seamstress
For the Director of Music. Of Sherye. A Psalm.

I carried my cell phone everywhere,
Waiting to hear from God.
He finally returned my call
And brought me much needed relief.
I was in so much trouble.
My debts piled high
From doctor and hospital bills.
I injured my hand and lost my job
When I went into the hospital.
I had no insurance,
So all the bills were mine to pay.
My boss would not rehire me,
I'd missed too many days.

The hospital wanted money,
My ex-friend wanted my job,
My ex-husband wanted the children –
To get back at me.
He hired himself a lawyer
With the money that he stole.
He took me to court
And I was about to lose.

Everyone turned their backs
Even my own parents.
My children lost respect
For their own mother.

It was God who took care of my bills,
He found angels to pay for them.
Another angel I had never met,
Talked to my boss,
Now I'm back at work,
Sewing as fast as I can.

I can't help but hum
A song of praise for Him.
As I sew up the seams
Of the beautiful dresses I make.

No longer is my employer
Mr. Famous Dressmaker
My boss is God Himself.
He always takes care of me.

I can't list all of the things
That God has done for me.
He has given daily food
For my children,
Health for my parents,
Who care for my children,
And a roof over all of our heads.
He protects me as I walk
Through the dark and dangerous streets
When I work late at night.

You don't desire personal sacrifice
But I give my self to You.
I no longer work for Mr. Famous Dream Maker
But for You.

I desire to do your will
To obey You in all things.
To be kind to my coworkers,
And to greet my employer with respect.
I will tell my neighbors all about You.
I will testify in church.

I had lost hope,
But then You rescued me
From complete despair.
I no longer have a debt
That I cannot pay.
My children have learned
To trust in You

And their father lost his battle
Against me in court.
The only debt I still owe
To You, my neighbors and enemies.
Is to love, love, love.
Praise God Hallelujah! Amen.

Psalm 41 For a Nurse's Healing
For the Director of Music. A Psalm of Sherye.

Happy is the nurse who cares for the sick
The Lord will care for her
As she cares for her patients.
She works hard long hours
But the Lord will protect her,
Give her long life and a strong back.
He will not allow the hospital
To take advantage of her.
If she gets ill herself the Lord will heal her.

I said, "Lord, heal my heart,
For I have sinned against You.
I have fallen in love with one of the patients,
Even though I'm married to the best man on earth.
The gossips were all saying,
"Someday she'll get caught,
Her husband will divorce her.
The hospital will fire her, too."

They said that I got sick
From all the stress of guilt.
"She got what she deserves."
My very best friend
No longer speaks to me.

Lord, have mercy on me.
Guilt for my sin never leaves me.
I have repented.
And no longer see that man.
I have confessed to my husband
He has forgiven me.
Please get me out of this hospital bed.

The Lord heard and forgave me.
He healed and restored my health.
I am back serving my patients.
Praise God, He forgives and forgets.
Praise His wonderful name.

BOOK II

Psalm 42 For a Broken Pastor

For the Director of Music. A Chorus by the Hanson Daughters.

As a runner pants for water,
So my soul pants for You. O God.
My soul thirsts for the living God
When is my next appointment with Him?
All I've eaten day and night
Are tears and sadness.
People ask me – "You're a Christian –
Doesn't God take care of you?"
I used to be a pastor
Who led the worship service.
The whole congregation
Listened to my sermons.
They sang the hymns that I chose
And responded by coming to the altar.
They told me how my words
Gave them a peace they'd never known.

Why are you depressed, Sherye?
What is your problem?
Trust in God.
For soon you will have cause
To praise Him,
My Savior Jesus Christ.

Depression weighs me down
Therefore I will think about You.
I'll remember when You brought me out
Of that deep depression
I had when my son was three.
Yet deeper down I go.
I can no longer get out of bed.

Daily He loves me through.
At night He comes into my thoughts.
I know He'll come for me.

I asked Jesus,
Did You forget me?
Have You put me on a shelf?
Why must I be depressed,
Because I am no longer a pastor.
My enemy tells everyone he can
What a terrible person I was.

Why are you depressed, Sherye?
What is your problem?
Trust in God
For you will soon have a reason
To praise Him.
Your Savior Jesus Christ.

Psalm 43 Where Are You?

Clear up the charges against me, o God.
Plead my case in an unjust court.
Rescue me from corrupt judges
And lying prosecutors.
You are my only defense –
Why didn't You show up in court?
Why must I go to trial in worry
Without an adequate defense?
Find a witness, and search for evidence,
Let them show me to be
Innocent of all the charges.
Then I will be free to go
To the altar and praise Your name.
I will sing on the platform
And praise You on the keyboard.
My wonderful God.

Don't worry, Sherye!
Don't be upset!
Put your trust in God,
For I know that I will praise Him
As my Savior and my God.

Psalm 44 Don't Forget About Us
For the Director of Music. A Chorus by the Hanson Daughters.

Our fathers told us
All about what You did for them.
A long time ago.
With Your hand
You gave this land to us
By driving out the nations.
You destroyed their enemies.
And built up our fathers.
They didn't win by themselves,
They couldn't fight a superior force.
It was only with Your help and Your guidance,
For You loved them.

You alone are my King and my God.
You announce victories for my nation.
With Your help we push back our enemies.
Through Your name we conquer them.
I don't trust in machine guns,
My assault rifle doesn't help me win.
You are the One who defeats them.
You send them away ashamed
We brag about You all day
And praise Your name forever.

But now You have let us lose
You no longer supply our armies,
With Your supernatural power.
We are forced to retreat
And they plunder from us.
We are eaten like sheep.
The nations have made our people
Prisoners of war everywhere.
You have sold us like slaves at an auction
Only pennies for each one of us.

Our neighbors think we're worthless
They laugh at our country.
You have make us the joke of all nations.
We no longer have any respect.

We are embarrassed at the United Nations.
The other countries scold us and scoff.
Our enemy gets all the glory
And they vote with that nation every time.

All of this happened
Even though we didn't forget You.
We worshipped in the temple.
We kept all the laws.
We love You with all of our heart.
Our feet had not strayed from Your path.

We are still Your people.
But You destroyed us and our land is empty of people.
Only wild dogs and rats live in the houses.

If we had forgotten You
And worshipped another god,
Wouldn't You have known?
You know all of our secrets?
Yet because of You we face death
Every day.
We are holocaust victims.

Wake up, Lord? Why are You sleeping?
Get up! Take care of us.
Why do You hide from Your people
And forget our oppression?

We are dust on the ground.
Our bodies are dried up.
Come and help us.
Defend us because of Your eternal love.

Psalm 45 Presidential Power

For the Director of Music. A Chorus by the Hanson Daughters.
A Song for the Inauguration.

I feel stirred to sing,
Praises for my president,
To carefully pick out words.

You are the best of the best
The Spirit has graced your word.
Since God has chosen you.
Dress in your finest suit,
Get in your newest limousine
With your secret service
Guarding you on every side.
Your generals display your wise plans
As you bomb the strategic sites
Of the Enemy.
May all the nations of the world
Respect your office and your power.

You have been chosen by the people
But God has allowed that you should be
Our first unelected president.
Chosen by decree.

God's sovereignty is eternal,
Justly, he reigns.
He loves the right and hates the wrong.

As you follow in His footsteps,
God has set you above all others.
You live in wealth and splendor.
The greatest musicians play for you.
Your wife is the first lady.

At the inaugural balls,
She will wear the finest gown.
Everyone will celebrate
Her beauty and her grace.
All the nations will come.
To ask for your favor.

The people of your party.
The friends from your state,
Hollywood and Harvard,
All will come to beg.

They will treat you like a king
Be careful of their praise.
Trust only in God.
Pray daily unto Him.
Ask Him for wisdom.

Be careful not to grasp power.
Do what's right for all.
Many people depend
On the decisions that you make.
Think peace instead of war.

Psalm 46 Our Shelter

For the Director of Music. A Chorus by the Hanson Daughters.

God is our shelter from the storm.
He runs a special emergency service.
We don't have to be afraid
Even in an earthquake high on
The Richter scale.
If the earth shifts and Mount Rainier blows
And the Green River fills with fallen trees.
We can call on you.
Though a tsunami floods the coast.
You will rescue us.

From the heart of God flows a river,
That flows into our hearts.
God dwells in our city.
God lives in our hearts

From morning until night.
Nations threaten,
Revolutions come.
God speaks.
All is silent.

The Mighty God is with us.
God is our powerful wall
He saves us from trouble
From both friend and enemy.

He makes peace in the midst of war.
He melts guns and digs up land mines.

Be quiet and be aware
That I am God
Over all the nations.
My rule extends over all the earth.

My reign reaches every nation.
The Mighty God is with us.
He is our source of Strength.

Psalm 47 God Reigns

For the Director of Music. A Chorus by the Hanson Daughters.

Clap your hands, all you nations;

Clap your hands and dance,
Sing and shout.
All nations of the earth.
God is the great King,
Wonderful in His awesome power.
He rules over all nations.
Yet He chose one nation
Out of all – to be His heritage.

Praise Him with joyful shouts.
Honor Him with trumpet sounds.
Sing praises to God, sing praises,
Sing praises to our King, sing praises.

God is the only King over all the earth.
He rules over all nations.
The ambassadors of all the nations
Assemble at the United Nations,
Not knowing that the earth belongs to God.
He is above all.

Psalm 48 Two Cities
A song. A psalm of Sherye.

God is great and worthy of all honor,
In our city, Seattle, and on Mount Rainier,
It is a beautiful mountain.
The city a beautiful city.
Yet it isn't God's city.

God's city is Jerusalem.
Torn by war and terror.
No longer do pilgrims come.
To worship God there.
For suicidal bombers
Who have nothing to lose.
Blow themselves up in cafes
And shopping centers.
The Israeli army invades
Arab houses and tears down their walls.

When, o God,
Are You going to come
And take back Your city.
Will it be after World War
When all the nations gather
To fight against Jerusalem?
Then will You return
And fight against all armies
And turn the Armageddon Valley
Into a River of Blood.

Why does it take war
To bring about peace
Why do people fight God
Instead of worship and praise.
How dreadful is that day.
Yet if You end all war.

Bring liberty and justice
From sin and oppression –
We will pay the price.
Your people are now scattered
Throughout the earth.
They follow You with joy.
Through this evil world.
Bring them to that city
The city of God.
A city of beauty and peace.

Psalm 49 Death
For the director of music. Of Sherye. A psalm.

Listen up, everyone,
To my report to the world
I exclude no one –
Rich or poor.
High or low.
I'm speaking to you all.

Why worry about monetary
Depressions, terror, and war,
When already we live in a world
Full of liars who depend on their stocks
And brag about their earnings?

No matter how rich you are,
Money cannot save you from death.
The price is too high.
Everybody dies,
Smart and dumb,
They all leave their wealth to others.
Their only house will be their grave.
Even though they have fancy estates
Named after themselves.

A human being, despite his riches,
Will not last.
He dies just like the animals.

Our fate, if we trust in ourselves,
And the fate of those we convince
Is that we all die.
Death eats us up like humanity eats meat.

Those who love the Lord will rule over
Those who trusted only in riches.

God will redeem us from death,
We will spend eternity with Him.

Don't be too impressed by the rich
And the luxury of his house.
For when he dies,
He will leave that house.
Even though he got special treatment
While he was alive,
Newspapers followed his every move,
He will die and lie in his grave.
A rich man without God
Will die like an animal.
His body will decay.
But I will be with Him
In Paradise.

Psalm 50 For Hypocrites
A psalm of Sherye.

Our Mighty God, The LORD brings summons
To all the earth from east to west
Out of Zion, the center of the earth,
God shines like the sun.
He comes in glory
With the beauty of the dawn,
And the wrath of the storm
He comes to judge His people.
Come to me,
All who made a covenant
With me, through Jesus Christ,
The ultimate sacrifice.
The angels, saints and elders
Preach to all of His justice.
God Himself is Judge.

Listen to me, o Christian,
I will testify against you.
You come to church
And sing hymns of praise.
You praise me with choruses.
You listen to a pious sermon
Wearing your best clothes.
You take the bread and wine.
Humbly confess your sins.
When things go wrong
You call on me.

I'm not angry about that.
What angers me is this.
When you take off
Your Sunday clothes.
You put on the clothes
Of a thief.

You celebrate your take,
With women in the bar.
While your wife sits at home.
You lie and deceive.
You speak against
Your brother.

I've seen all of this
But haven't called you on it.
I won't be patient forever.
If you really believe in me.
Then repent and follow me.
Practice what you pray.
Honor me with your deeds.
Or I will destroy you.
For I am God.

Psalm 51 Cleanse me

After I had an affair I prayed this psalm.
This poem reflects the guilt I felt then.

God, I have sinned, please forgive me.
I know that I have nothing to offer You.
You love me because of who You are.
Please cleanse my dirty heart
And scrub away the guilt.

I'm aware that what I did was wrong.
I can never forget it – day or night.
I have sinned against You,
Not just my lover and myself.
You are right to judge me.
I was born a sinner,
And have been a sinner ever since.
You desire that I be honest
Teach me to think Your way, Lord.

Cleanse me with pumice and I will be clean.
Scrub me with a loofah till the dead skin is gone.
Let me feel the comfort of Your strong hands
As You massage away the guilt.
Cover me with soft clothing
And hide my shame.

Create in me a soft heart like Yours, O God.
Give me stability in the face of temptation.
Don't send me away from Your house
Or take Your Holy Spirit from me.
Give me back my joy
I need a teachable heart, Lord,
So that I can learn.

Then I will teach sinners
As You have taught me.

Save me from my guilt.
My Savior and I will sing
Of Your mercy and kindness.
You don't want sacrifices.
What You want is a broken heart,
One that is willing to repent and change.

Let me be able to do Your will
And build up the Kingdom of God.
So that others may know of Your
Mercy and love.
Truth and power.

Psalm 52 Betrayal

For the music director. A dirge by David.

Why do you brag about your betrayal.
You wicked man.
You whose work God despises?
Your tongue's only use is destruction.
You sharpen it on a stone,
So that your words will be much stronger.
You love to hurt rather than heal;
Love lies more than the truth;
And love to dig with your words.

God will certainly get you.
He will take you while you're young.
You will go to an early death.

No one will miss you.
Everyone will be relieved.
A destructive man lies in the grave,
Who only wanted to destroy.

Your tomb will say,
"Here lies a man
Who depended on Himself
And got rich exploiting others."

I am like the apple tree
Flourishing in my backyard.
It grows with only God's attention.
Producing fruit from year to year.

I trust in God's eternal love.
I praise Him for His care.
In His Good Name I will hope.
I will praise Him in the presence of His people.
Thank You, God.

Psalm 53 More Than Consumers
For the music director.

The corporate man says to himself,
"There is no god but me.
I make up the rules,
And no one can touch me."

God searches to find one
Among humanity.
Who understands His ways,
And seeks to do His will,
But He finds no one.
Everyone has gone his own way.
They corrupted themselves with wealth.

Will those who disobey God ever learn –
Those who treat people like consumers
And manipulate them to buy things they do not need?
They will meet their end in the next recession.
When consumers decide to no longer buy
But live with what they have.
All the corporate structure will collapse
In a heap of greed and corruption.

Oh, that we would see a new day, when people
Are treated as people and all worship the Lord,
When God fills our spirits with joy and love
Instead of consumer goods.

Psalm 54 Rescue Me
For the Music Director. With guitars. By Sherye

Rescue me, for I'm in danger.
My enemy found me
And wants to kill me.
I wish him no harm,
But he envies me.

He hired killers to kill me.
People who don't care about God.
Only You, Lord, can rescue me.

I know, Lord, that You have helped me.
I've seen the enemy when he hasn't seen me.
You've been a shield about me.
Hiding me from him and his killers.

I wish that they would get what they deserve,
But You have said that I should be like You.
One who loves His enemies
And prays for them who persecute Him.

I will serve You night and day.
I will praise Your holy name,
For You have rescued me from harm.
You have saved me from my enemies.

Psalm 55 I Lost My Best Friend
For the director of music. With stringed instruments. A Ballad of Sherye.

Listen to me, Lord,
Don't ignore me.
Please hear me out.
Give me an answer.
I'm sad and depressed
The accuser in my head tells me "I'm no good."
People on the street turn their heads and stare.
I feel scared and alone.
It seems like everyone hates me.

I'm afraid to die.
And tremble at the thought of death.
Horrible thoughts come into my head,
Thoughts of violence and disease.
I said, "If only I could fly away
And find a peaceful nest
Far away from here
In the desert all alone.
I would fly on the air currents
And speed my way home.
Away from the storm."

Lord, invade this city
Full of violence and fear.
Let Your spirit come and bring
Peace to all who live here.
Drugs and crime are all around.
Indifference is all we feel.
We are no longer neighbors
But strangers here.

If it were an outsider who was bothering me.
I could understand.
But it is my very best friend,

Who has deserted me.
We were always in each other's houses.
Shopping and eating out.
We would talk on the telephone
If we weren't together.

Why are you now my enemy?
Why do you talk behind my back?
Everyone thinks that I've done
Something wrong.
Why can't you come to me
And talk it out?

But for some reason you refuse.
I must let you go.

I must trust in God to make things right again.

Psalm 56 I Feel Like A Failure

What can I do, Lord?
I feel like I'm surrounded
By people who refuse to understand me.
They aren't my enemies.
Yet they block my path.
I volunteer to work at church
And they refuse to let me do anything
Except bake cookies.

I have a Master of Divinity
And was on the way to being a pastor.
But now I cannot even teach Sunday School.
They support me with prayer
But only by telling me to give up.
I feel like they would like to see me fail.
I know that there is nothing I can do
To change their minds.

On the other hand, all of Jan's recovery friends
Think that I am crazy.
We did something you're not supposed to do.
We bailed out someone who wronged us.
They are certain that we are enabling him
To continue to use drugs without consequence.

I feel like a fool sometimes
Blundering through life.
I try to work at writing
But so far I've had no response.
It is a career almost guaranteed to fail.
There are so few who succeed.
Why is it that I'm always going uphill
And upstream instead of taking the easy road?

Yet I know deep in my heart,
That I am where You want me to be.
Doing something that is very hard
And probably will not work.
There is no guarantee.
The odds are against it.
Yet my job is to follow You
And if I fail – then only You
Will know what is gained from it.
No longer do I feel sorry for myself.
I am in the center of Your will.

Psalm 57 In Civil War

For the music director. By Sherye

I'm an so afraid, Lord,
This is such a dangerous time.
Our neighbors all have had
Their houses broken into
There are drug deals conducted
On the sidewalk in front of my house.
Last month someone was murdered
On my street.

I call the police
But they do nothing.
I'm afraid a crack house
Has moved next door.
There are cars that come in and out.
I write down all their license plates.
My neighbors do, too.
Yet when we call the police.
They say there is nothing they can do.

So God, here I am praying.
Please clean up my neighborhood.

Dear child,
Don't you know that all those
Who buy and sell are my creation.
That I died to save them from their sin.
Pray for them and love them.
Bake cookies and give them some.
They may be drug addicts
But they are still children.
They may be dealers
But there is a piece of their heart.
Not totally sold out to sin.
Your Savior

Dear Jesus,
The one who died for me.
I will praise You to all I meet.
I will send them cookies in Your name.
And bow down on my knees.
I will ask what I can do.
To be Your messenger on earth.
Your child.

Psalm 58 Against Crooked Politicians
For the Music Director. Of Sherye.

Do you politicians tell the truth?
Do you judges make fair decisions?
No, you care only for those
Who are rich enough to contribute
And the middle class who will vote.
You care nothing for the poor.

If a poor man breaks the law,
He spends months in jail.
If he doesn't pay his fine.
He is put in jail again.
If a rich man breaks the law.
His lawyer gets him off.
He pays a fine he can afford.
He worries not about the cost.

I wish that I could write the laws.
And send the corporation lobbyists
Out of town.
They want it all and if they don't get it,
Take their teams out of town,
Build their factories out of the country.
They do not care about the working man or woman.

I know that I would waste my time
Running for office.
So I will complain
And I will pray.
That the Lord's justice will prevail.
That those who poison the water, soil and air.
Will get their just reward.
Those who steal because they're hungry
Will find relief.

116

Reward those who serve You.
O God, who judges the earth.

Psalm 59 For the Debtor

For the music director. When I was hounded by creditors.

Deliver me from my creditors, o God,
They hound me day and night.
I stopped paying my telephone bill
So they would no longer call me.
Then they sent debt collectors to my house
And told me they were going to take me
To court if I didn't pay.

It would be different if I'd gone on
Charge account shopping sprees,
Or had gambled all my money.
I don't own a car.
I rent the cheapest place in town.
I work two jobs.
I made a payment plan with the hospital.
But they sent me to collections anyway.
They said that I'll never pay
A half-million-dollar debt
At fifty dollars a month.

That is probably true.
But all the rest of my money
Goes to child support.
My children have to eat
And have a roof over their head.
Their mother may have her problems
But she works hard.
She was about to go under, too,

When I had the accident.
I fell off a ladder onto my back.
One of my vertebrae broke
And I still suffer from pain.

118

I can still work but I can't work overtime.
And work security instead.
If I quit and go on disability.
The hospital won't get a dime.
I don't understand why they did this to me.

It's not the collectors' fault –
They are just doing their job.
In fact, when I told them the situation
They were sympathetic.

But the hospital, what's their excuse?
They buy every new piece of equipment
That comes on the market.
They kept asking me about insurance,
I told them I don't have any.
They didn't believe me.
Then they got mad
Because the ambulance
Came to the nearest hospital
Instead of the county one.

The ambulance driver drove me there
Because in addition to breaking my back.
He feared I also had a heart attack.
Sometimes I wished I'd died.

Last time I saw my children,
I couldn't wrestle with them anymore.
I told them I was sorry,
But my sweet little daughter said,
With the most serious face,
"I don't care, Daddy, I'm so glad you are alive.
I wouldn't like living without a Daddy."
My son, who is the shy and silent type,
Came to me, gave me a big hug
And said, "All I want is for you to be here."
Tears came to my eyes
I saw what a wonderful God You are,
You saved my life.

I'll give You thanks
And leave the creditors to You.

Psalm 60

This the prayer of George Patton,
Who didn't understand what
God was doing with the weather,
Just before the Battle of the Bulge.

Sir,
I am General Patton, speaking to you.
The past fourteen days on the battlefield,
Have been like hell.
Rain, snow, more rain, more snow –
What are you doing at headquarters?
Whose side are you on anyway?
Damn faith and patience!
You must come to my aid,
So I may dispatch
the entire German army
By Christmas,
Which is by the way,
The birthday of Your prince of peace.
Sir, I have never been an unreasonable man,
I am asking the impossible.
I request four days of clear weather.

There was silence in heaven.
The bad weather continued.
I was unable to fight.
Then the reports came in.

Sir, this is Patton again,
I beg to report complete progress.
Sir, it seems to me
that You had better information than I,
You knew that the weather
Which I commanded You to change,
Made the entire German army
Commit suicide.

That, sir, was a brilliant military move,
I bow humbly to a supreme military genius.

Psalm 61 A Legislator's Prayer
Prayer from a Congressman

Do you hear me, God?
I'm on my knees begging for help.

I'm as far away from You
As I can get
And I'm in trouble.
Lead me to a place
That is above me
And my problems.
In the past You were
Always there for me
I could always count on You

I look forward to the day when
I can live with You forever.
Whether in a small apartment
Or a mansion in the sky.
I made promises to You
That I didn't keep.
You made promises to me
And have kept every one.

When I ran for office
I forgot about You.
I gave in to the lobbyists
And the voters too.
But now that I have been elected,
Could You spare my life,
So I'll have many days of service
To my country and to You.
Then I'll sing Your praises
And fulfill my vows I made
Before You to my country.

Psalm 62 Heart Transplant

For the music director. A Psalm of Sherye
For Bill and Scott

There's only one place where I can rest,
The presence of the Lord.
He saved me, healed me and set me free.
All of my serenity comes from Him.
I hide in His arms.

How long will this time of trouble be?
When will there be peace for my family.
Wave after wave of hard things come.
The enemy only wants us to fail.
Our friends think we're foolish.
Strangers think that we're wrong.
Only in You can we stay strong.

I am tired, I need to rest.
Only in God will I find peace.
You will save all the others who live in my house.
You will heal them and set them free.
All of us can pour out our hearts to You.
We can complain of all our problems
And You always listen.
Your door is always open.
Your office hours are 24/7.

The poor die in a minute
And the rich live a lie.
If all that we did was written down,
It would amount to nothing.
Do not trust in fraud,
Or brag about the things you stole,
Though you may have nice things,
Don't depend on them.

God's invisible justice is working,
He will reward us all
According to what we have done.
You are just and merciful.
We just need to ask.
You forgive and wipe out our sins
And give us a heart transplant.
Our lying, cheating, thieving heart
You replace with a clean one
Full of love for You.

Psalm 63 A Mother's Prayer

A psalm of a mother seeking help for her daughter.

O God, You are my God,
I asked for prayer for my daughter;
On Sunday night in church,
My heart longs for an answer,
My body is weary without sleep
I am in the land without mercy
For the mentally ill.

I have seen You in the cathedral,
I have beheld Your glory in the forest
And Your power in the ocean.
You have so much love for me
That I'd rather die than live without You.
I will praise You all my life
And with my entire being
I will be happy loving You.
When I eat at Your table, I am full and filled
With the finest food that can be prepared.
I will sing about You all day long
Even though I annoy the neighbors with my song.

When I'm in the E.R. I will remember You.
I will think of You as I wait for the doctor.
Because You are my help.
I sing under the protection of Your loving hand.
When all other hope is gone
I hang on to the knowledge
That You have not forgotten us.

Those who refuse to help will find the door
Shut upon them when they seek help.
They will find out that their callous hearts
Will be brought into court.

126

But we will find the help we need.
You will open doors that were shut before.
You will help at the proper time.
You are a just-in-time sort of God.

Psalm 64 Injustice System
For the music director A psalm of Sherye.

Listen, God, to the formal complaint,
I will write unto the legislators.
I am tired of the injustice system
That rules over criminals
Who are poor.

They get caught up into the system
And can never get out.
One crime is punished three times,
Because nothing changes
And so they continue to commit crimes.
Work is impossible.
Living on the streets,
Stealing, using drugs and driving
Without a license,
Getting caught again and again.
Failure to appear.
Gets added again.

Crime and jail becomes a never-ending cycle.
During all this time.
They have committed no violence.
They use drugs to deaden the pain.
And steal to buy the drugs.
They drive without a license to
Get to where they are going.

Nothing is done to change this cycle.
Just jail and more jail.
If they would compare the price of treatment.
With the price of courts and jail.
They would find they are saving money.

Then they are to sign up for treatment.
With many hurdles to jump
And end up with treatment.
Two days a week.
With their only reward a punishment.
Do they care about outcome?
Do they want success?
No, they only want to process
Another man or woman through
The system of injustice.

God, my prayer to You is this,
That You would send a message to the legislators.
Tell them that if they want justice
To reform the system
And make it fair for all.
Make them see these drug addicts
As human beings and not just cases,
To be processed, jailed and put on probation –
Where failure is likely
And success is unusual.
Tell the judges who throw the book
That their way is not working.
Tell the legislature
That building more jails is not the answer.
Remind them to show mercy
And provide a means of escape.
That the revolving door will go
Only one way out and send into society
A changed man or woman.
Only You can change the hearts.
So this is my plea,
Make my complaint
Powerful to every legislator.

Psalm 65 God Our Savior
For the Music Director. By Sherye Hanson.

We have nothing but praise for You, o God.
The vows we made, we will fulfill.
You are the One who hears our prayers.
All humanity comes to You.
When we suffer from guilt
For our numberless sins,
You forgive us.
The happiest people are those
Who live in heaven with You.
Even here and even now,
We live in Your Kingdom on earth.

When we tell You our needs,
You answer us with miracles.
You save us and give us hope.
Even those far away,
Across the oceans,
You have not left out.
With Your strong arm,
You shaped the mountains.

You quiet the roaring seas,
And the conflict between nations.
Those who live far way
Are aware of Your gifts.
The beautiful dawn and the gorgeous sunset
Sing of Your wonderful love.

The rain that waters the earth
Is Your production.
The grain that feeds us
Is Your doing.
You drench the land,
Level the soil,

Soften it with showers
And make the crops grow.
Every year You bring in the harvest
Which is more than enough.
The desert grasslands
Are green with new grass.
Sheep that cover the hillsides
And grain that fills the valleys,
Sing joyfully to our God.

Psalm 66 To Praise God
A Song.

Sing and shout to God, all you peoples.
Sing the glory of His name.
Say to God, "How great is Your power."
Sing to God the glory of His name.
Rebellious nations bow before You.
All earth kneels down in awe of You.
Sing glory to His name
Sing praises to His name.
Hallelujah.

Look at what our God has done,
See how awesome are His works.
Notice the land raised up from sea.
How awesome are His works.
Israel passed on a path through the water,
God rules forever by His power.
His eyes watch over all the nations.
Rebellious peoples must obey Him.
Praise the Lord.

Praise God, o nations of the earth,
Sing your praises to be heard.
He kept us safe and saved our lives,
Sing your praises loud and strong.
You, o God, have tested us,
Thrown us into prison and hard labor,
Sent men to conquer us,
Through fire and water taken us.
Thank the Lord.

I will keep my promises
That I made to You in church
And in the middle of the fire
I will keep the promise made to You in worship.

I will give my life to You.
I surrender all I have.
All I own is Yours to use.
My body, my wealth and my time.
Amen.

Everyone, listen to what I have to say,
Let me tell what God has done.
I cried out to Him in pain,
Let me tell how God has saved me.
If I had disobeyed my God,
He would not have listened to me.
Since I did all He told me to
God has heard my prayer for help.
Hurrah!

Psalm 67 A Praise Song
A simple song

Be generous, kind, and enjoy us.
Spread the news about Your ways.
Show the nations Your salvation.
Command praise from all people.
Teach all people to enjoy the Lord.
Guide every tribe upon the earth.

Then the land will yield harvests,
God will certainly provide for us,
And all nations on the earth will honor the Lord.

Psalm 68 God and America
A Song Of Sherye Concerning the Pilgrims to Modern Times

God will stand up against His enemies.
They will scatter in all directions.
They will dissipate like smoke
And die in the battle.
God's friends will be happy and joyful.

Sing to God, sing praises to His name,
While He rides on the clouds,
He is God,
Enjoy Him.
He is Father to those without fathers,
And defends widows from predators,
To those who are alone, He provides families.
God releases prisoners with song,
But rebels live in the desert.

When You sailed with Your people
Across the Atlantic,
They suffered through violent storms.
Finally they found a safe place to land.
Where they suffered many illnesses,
Many graves were filled there,
And they had trouble growing food.

You sent a native of the land.
To teach them how to grow corn,
To fish and hunt and care for themselves.
They made Massachusetts, the colony, their home.
Others followed and You provided for them as well –
The rich and the poor.

Then a hundred or more years later,
Fed up with taxes and foreign kings,
They declared their independence.

Through a volunteer army with little pay
And not enough food.
They won against the British army
Who gave up and withdrew.
They left a government of rule by the people
And created their own Constitution.

The United States Army grew in strength and ability
And became the power that the nations called on
When they needed help.
The nation established itself "Under God,"
And stamped on its coins "In God we trust."
Praise God that we live in a land that is free,
Prosperous and generous,
You have saved us through mighty wars,
And brought us into peace.

Many nations envy us.
Some would go to war.
Since they aren't strong enough.
They fight us with terror.

As we parade down the streets
And celebrate our freedom
With bands, and singers,
And dancing in the streets.
Remind us of Your love and power
From tiny Rhode Island to giant Alaska.

Show Your strength to us.
Because of the power of Washington,
And the wealth of New York.
Many come bringing gifts.
Command all the nations
That prefer war to peace.
To submit themselves to God
We may be the most powerful nation
On earth right now.
Remind us that You are greater than us.
Don't let us forget to call upon You for strength.

To rule wisely and not throw our power around.
We must submit to the Lord,
And praise and honor Him.
For the many gifts He has given to us.
You are the One who deserves honor,
Not us with all our armies.
We owe all we have to You.
You are the mighty One.
We are weak and powerless before You.
Praise be to God!

Psalm 69 For Christmas 2002

For the music director. By Sherye Hanson.

Today, o God,
I need Your help,
For I am overwhelmed with problems.
My daughter, Britta, is in the hospital.
I have a stomach ache that won't go away.
It's Christmas and I don't feel like celebrating.
Bill needs to get into treatment.
Scott will soon go to jail.
Janaee has to get into a training program.
Kristina wants to go shopping.
Kurt is tired and worried.

Right now it doesn't seem
Like Christmas.
The house is dirty.
My desk a mess.

How can I be helping others
When I can hardly help myself.
I cry for no reason.
I explode at anything.
I haven't sent cards
Or Christmas letters.
All I can do is go to church,
Sing carols and listen to sermons –
About a pregnant Mary,
A worried Joseph,
And a terrible king.

So even though no one understands,
And our household is either sick
Or depressed,
I pray that as we celebrate Christmas
With a couple of homeless kids,

We will remember Your great love.
Your love has carried us through
Other hospitalizations,
Other times in jail.
Other school failures.

Deliver us from fear
Bring us joy and laughter.
Remind us of our salvation in You.

Come and rescue us.
Find Britta the right medication
To clear her psychotic thinking
And level her moods.
Find Bill and bring him home.
Comfort Scott while he's away from family
Give Janaee joy with Dad
And Sandi fun with her grandpa.
Help us to clean the house,
Fix the meals.
Find the right presents.

Above all restore our house
To cleanliness and sanity.
That we may celebrate together
Your holy birth.

When Christmas is a difficult time.
I remember You.
Your life was never easy
From conception to the grave.
Yet through Your divine love.
You overcame it all.

Christmas is the promise
Of God's invasion of earth.
You invaded the hard places.
You saved the difficult people.
You healed the impossible cases

So bring our family into Your loving care.
Help us to remember to not be afraid,
But to trust in You to deliver us
From the enemies of illness,
Drugs and past sins.
In Your wonderful name
I pray, Amen

Psalm 70 Save Me from My Craving

For the music director. By Sherye. A request.

Hurry up, God.
I need Your help now,
Not tomorrow.
I crave the drug so much.
I want to go out and use.
I don't want to go
To another meeting
And confess that I have slipped.
I am so ashamed of myself.
I want to be strong.
Please listen to me.
Give me the sobriety
Of those who claim to have
Weeks and Months and Years.

They give You all the credit
And so will I
I'm in trouble, Lord,
Weak and afraid.
Please come
I need You now.
Take away this desire.
Replace it with Your love.

Psalm 71 For My Gray Hair

I am hidden in You.
Save me, Lord.
Be my hiding place
Where I can always go,
Say the word,
And I will be saved.
My Enemy chases after me.
Deliver me.

You are my hope, Ruler of the Universe,
I trusted in You when I was a baby,
You stood by the doctor
When he delivered me.
Thank You, Lord.
I am alive.
For some You are a threat,
But for me You are a tent,
To keep out of the rain.
I can't stop praising You.
You are so beautiful, my God.

When I get old, don't forget about me.
Even though I will be too weak to serve You.
My Enemy hides and waits for me,
He wants to kill me.
His friends say, "God doesn't love her anymore.
Let's get her, for she has no one to protect her."

Keep close to me
Watch over my life.
May my enemies
– Illness, poverty and frail bones –
Stay far from me.

In You I will put my hope.
I will praise You more each day.
I will tell all my neighbors,
And grandchildren all about You.
I will tell all the things You've done for me.
From youth until now You've been my teacher.
So now that I'm old and gray,
Don't leave me.
Let me live long enough
To tell the next generation
Of Your power
To heal, save and protect.

Your justice and mercy are higher than heaven,
You have done great things.
Who in earth or heaven is like You.
Greater than the universe,
Yet born as a human baby,
Living among us as a man.
Teaching us about Your love.
Then dying to save us from our sins,
Living again to bring us up from death.

Though I've lived a difficult life.
You will bring me up from death.
I will rise from the grave
In a new body.
You will bring me to heaven
To live with You
In honor and comfort.

If I could play that piano
And sing for You, I would.
If I could play the guitar
And harmonize,
I'd sing in front of church
But You know that I can only sing
With the congregation,
I will sit in front of church.
And sing as loud as I can,

SHERYE HANSON

For You have delivered me
From fear of death.
I am Your child.
Glory Hallelujah!

Psalm 72 President Clinton

Some rulers disappoint. Solomon came to office with a lot of promise. Bill Clinton did too. But both men failed God and their nation. Despite his failure, God was faithful to Israel. God will be faithful to us. Will we be faithful to Him?

After twelve long years of Republicans.
We want a President who will bring back justice,
Who will appoint supreme court judges
That favor the poor as well as the rich.
Our economy has gone sour
And so we ask that You bring prosperity.
We pray that he will provide
Universal health insurance for every single person.
He will take care of children on welfare,
And prosecute those who harm the children.
May he serve two terms and be followed.
By another Democrat.
He will be a fresh breath of air
After those corrupt Republicans.
In his days those who are oppressed will flourish.

His power will extend beyond our national borders.
He will be the most powerful man in the world.
Both Arab and Jew will respect him.
He will bring peace to the middle east.
Europe, Latin America, Asia and Africa
Will bring gifts to him.
Canada and Britain will become his best friends.
Even Mexico will desire his aid.
All the prime ministers, presidents, and premiers
Of the earth will come to him for help.

He will deliver those on welfare.
Those without insurance will have insurance.
He will save those who have no hope
By giving them hope.

Make sure he remains in office for eight long years.
We want the party to be prosperous when he is in office.
Tell the people to pray for him so that he will make wise decisions.
Above all, encourage him to turn to You
And Your pastors when times get rough.
Help him to endure criticism about his past.
Keep him from sinning his habitual sins.
Forgive him for the past and strengthen him in the future.

So that Your name will be praised.
This is the prayer of the Democratic Party.

BOOK III

Psalm 73 Envy
A Psalm of Sherye.

God certainly is good to His people,
The ones who do what's right.

But I almost slipped and fell.
For I envied the drug dealers

When I saw how well they lived.
They have no troubles.

They sleep until noon.
They don't commute at rush hour.

They wear the finest clothes,
Drive the nicest car,
Go out with the prettiest women.

They have no feelings,
And no conscience.

They cut you down in a second,
And threaten the lives of all who interfere.

They promise heaven on earth to their customers
Many buy a good time and freedom from pain.

They say, "God doesn't care
About what I do – He doesn't stop me!"

This is what the drug dealers are like
They have no worries, they get richer every day.

It's stupid of me to do what's right,
To go to work each day.

My back is sore, my knees are bad,
I can't take this anymore.

I could say, "I'll talk like them
And pretend that God doesn't care."

However, I would betray my wife,
My children and myself.
Still, the money sure does sound good.

But then I went to church
And heard the preacher say,

"I was a drug dealer once,
I spent a long time in prison.

"At first the life seems great,
And then I feared everyone.

"Someone down the street
Is waiting to set you up.

"Every customer is a narc.
There is no one I could trust.

"Then one day it happens,
Arrest, jail and trial.

"Before I knew it,
I was in for five to ten.

"My girl left me for another,
I knew my life was over.

"Then I heard a preacher
Who came into my cell.

"He told me of God's love
He came into my heart.

"Sinner sitting in the pew,
Give your life to Jesus.

"He will always be with you.
And hold you in His hands.

"He will guide you
And take you into glory."

I said to myself
As I listened to him,

"Whom do I have but You, God?
Nothing on earth or heaven.

"My body and spirit may be broken,
But God will give me strength.

"Those who are still on the street,
Will all eventually die.

"I will be with You.
You always keep Your promise."

Psalm 74 About Our Family
A complaint by Sherye Hanson

Why does it seem, God, like You've rejected our family?
Why do You get mad at us all the time?
Remember that we made our vows before You.
Reverend Timothy Ashley married Kurt and me in church.
We have been faithful to each other.
Yet the enemy would destroy our daughters if he could.

What about the people who live in our house, Lord?
They continue to be punished for the same crime.
It takes an enormous amount of work to get into treatment,
Whether for chemical dependency or mental illness
There are barriers all the way.

Janaee went to school with enthusiasm
But three days before she finished she was kicked out.
Scott has to go to jail because he committed more crimes.
Even though he was punished before
For that crime and all of the other ones.

Why is their no justice for the mentally ill and the chemically dependent?
Doesn't our family count with You?
Can't You break through and supply the needs of our family members?
Why do You allow the enemy to continue to harass us?

You are the Eternal God, who brought us salvation.
You redeemed us from sin when You died on the cross.
You broke the head of Satan when You rose from the dead.
You took the sting out of Death when You came back to life.

You opened streams of living water
When You sent Your Spirit on the church at Pentecost.
You created time – day and night,
Seasons – fall, winter, spring and summer.

The enemy still walks upon the earth,
Like a lion seeking something to eat.
Protect us from temptation.
Save us from the Evil One.

Psalm Song 75 God and Our Nation

For the Music Director. A psalm of Sherye
To be sung on Memorial Day

Thank You, God, for being close to us.
Thank You that we can call on Your name
And You will perform miracles.

You tell us, "I'll be on time,
Let me be the judge,
When an earthquake comes
And everyone is afraid,
I will hold the foundations firm.

To the arrogant I say, "Shut up and listen."
To the powerful I say, "Who do you think you are? God?
I am the One and Only God."

There is no one anywhere who can promote anyone.
Only God, who decides,
He makes one man poor, and one woman rich.
He forces the crooked man to suffer for His crimes.

As for me, I will tell the story of the God
Who saved our nation,
Who defeated our enemies.
And will give us victory if we promote justice.

Satan doesn't want to give up his children.
Save each of our family members from him.
May they be born into God's Kingdom.
Into God's protection and care.

Remember the salvation You brought through Jesus.
Make true the good news to the poor.
That Scott, Bill and Janaee may stay clean,
Get jobs and contribute to the needs of the poor.

That Kristina and Britta may be healed
Go to school and work for Your Kingdom.

Stand up, God, and defend our cause
Before the legislature and those in power
Both on the earth and in the spiritual realm.
We pray in Jesus' name. Amen.

Psalm 76 Two Churches
By Sherye Hanson

In Rainier Avenue Free Methodist Church,
We worship God.
In Living Hope Community Fellowship,
Your name is great.

You do not live in these churches,
But You live in the hearts of those who worship there.
When they go home, to school and to work,
You go with them.

You, o Lord, are full of light,
Your glory makes Mount Rainier seem small.
Your enemies of sin and death
Have been defeated.
They lie still within the grave.

If God is for us, who can be against us?
If we disobey You, then we are alone in our disobedience.
Lord, we dedicate ourselves to You.
Help us to be honest in our vows.

Let those who live near us
Come to see what You are doing here
At Rainier Avenue and Living Hope.
Mother and daughter churches.

Psalm 77 A Psalm About Depression
For the music director.
Dedicated to Britta

Last night I cried myself to sleep.
I prayed to God but He didn't answer.
My broken heart could not be healed.
I stretched out my hands to You
But You didn't grasp them.

This morning when I woke up,
I remembered my first suicide attempt.
After I got out of the hospital
I went to church.
Where I heard good news
For the first time.
I found out that
I didn't have to seek for You.
You already found me.
All I needed to do was to say,
"Yes."
At the moment, I remained in my pew.
But when the preacher prayed,
I said,
"Yes."

Another time, another hospital
When I was
Being treated for depression,
The doctor confronted me
I listened and You performed a miracle.
I left the hospital with hope.
Went out and got a job.
Studied hard and finished a degree.
Three years later I found a good job.

Throughout all my depressions,
You were there.
You brought me out of the pit of despair
And set me up on top of the mountain of joy.

When I see my daughter
Suffering from bipolar,
I remember that what You did for me
You can do for her.
The depths of depression,
And the heights of mania,
Are not to hard for You.
You are the Great Physician,
You can heal my daughter.
I don't have to be afraid.
Though I may not see
Your invisible hand.
You are there
Guiding the doctor
And comforting my daughter.

Psalm 78 A Family History

God chose His people
And has not abandoned them.

He chose Israel to be His own
And put up with them
From Abraham unto Jesus.
Then Jesus ushered in a new Kingdom.
This Kingdom was not based
On being the descendent of Abraham –
But being born into the Kingdom of God
By believing in Jesus' name.

Just as the history of Israel is
One of disobedience and shame
As well as obedience and accomplishment,
So too, the church.

The first generation of Christians were
Chosen by Jesus to be His twelve disciples.
He chose also seventy to proclaim His Word.
That generation received the Holy Spirit
And went throughout the Roman world
And spread the good news.
Some believed and were saved.
They were added into the Kingdom of God.
The Judaizers wanted to combine
The Old Testament law
With the New Covenant of Christ.
They made trouble for the Gentiles
Leading Paul to condemn them publicly.

Others sought to mix the faith
With pagan ideas.
They found the thought that Christ took on
Human flesh repulsive

And believed in a spiritual Christ.
They denied the body,
Labeled the body as sin and the spirit as holy.
Many people followed this belief
And lost their understanding of Jesus Christ.
The first generation died.
Many were martyrs of the faith.
Of the twelve disciples, only one
Died a natural death.

The church continued to be persecuted
Sporadically by the pagan emperors of Rome.
Finally Deius came and persecuted
Christians throughout the empire,
Valerian took away Christians' property,
Then under Diocletian and Glaerius,
Churches were destroyed, Bibles burned.
Sacrifice to gods was required.

The church continued and grew,
The next generation also suffered and died.
This continued until the Emperor Constantine
Became a Christian
And made the faith the state religion.

He worshipped in large pagan temples
And so he built large churches
With the same design.
The simple early church that met in homes,
Rented halls, and river banks
Became a building
Where people went and watched a priest
Perform the sacrament of communion.

A church that had worshipped in the synagogue tradition
Became a church that worshipped in the pagan tradition
Of a temple, priest and sacrifice.

The church fought against heresy.
Some Jews didn't believe Jesus was God

Only a human Messiah.
Greeks found the idea of God being
Born in a human body impossible.
They didn't believe Jesus was really human.
Others thought Satan and Christ equals
And it was unknown as to whether
Good would win over evil.

These controversies continued where
Christians debated the nature of Jesus Christ.
Councils agreed on creeds.
At Nicea where the creed was born,
Constaninople, where the Trinity was decided.
At Ephesus Pelagius and the Nestorians were
Found to be heretics.
At Chalcedon Christ's two natures were
Declared unmixed.
Constaninople had two more councils
And finally it was at Nicea the council legitimized
Icons and statues.
The New Testament Canon was formed.

During this time the gospel continued to spread.
The Goths, Picts, Irish, Franks, Scots, Angles
Saxons and Frisians were converted.

The eastern church went to the Slavic peoples
And invented Cyrillic.

The church at Rome became very powerful
And the Bishop of Rome became Pope
Of all the church.

As the centuries passed,
The Eastern and Western church
Went separate ways.
Then an envoy of the Pope
Insulted Patriarch Michael Geularius
Pope Leo and Patriarch Michael
Excommunicated each other in 1084.

Monks created orders to clean up the church.
First came the Benedictines,
Then the Knights of John
Knights Templar defended
Pilgrims to Jerusalem.
Teutonic knights created hospitals
In the Holy Land.
Cluniacs reformed the Benedictines.
Cisterians went even further.
Augustinians followed Augustine.
Along with the Premonstrants of France.
Carthusians flagellated themselves.
Carmelites began on Mount Carmel.
St. Teresa of Avila joined this order.
Dominicans rooted out heresy.
Franciscans took a vow of poverty.
Jesuits fought the Counter Reformation.

During this era, the church fought
Crusades against the Muslims.
Christians wanted to keep the Holy Land
In Christian hands.
There were seven crusades.
Some succeeded, others did not.
The children's crusade resulted in the death
And slavery of the children.

At the lowest point of the church,
The cardinals chose popes from powerful families.
For fifty years, Avignon appointed popes,
In addition to the Roman popes.
Then, in an effort to reform the process,
Church councils appointed popes.

Then God sent men within the church,
Who protested church corruption.
The most well-known were John Wycliff,
John Huss, Girolano Savonarola and
Desiderius Erasmus.

Then Luther came and reformed the church,
He split with the church
And formed the Lutheran Church
Then Zwingli in Switzerland,
John Calvin in France,
John Knox in Scotland
Formed national churches
Outside the dominion of the pope.
With radical reform of theology and clergy,
The Anabaptists – Hutterites, Mennonites and
Amish formed Free Churches
Outside the national church.
With the church split into pieces,
War broke out between the mother
Church and her illegitimate daughters.

Within the reformation,
The Arminians and Calvinists disputed
Salvation at five points.

Puritans followed Presbyterians,
They went to America,
Within the Freedom of America,
Many other denominations formed.
They grew and prospered.
Through revivals they became powerful.

In the twentieth century,
The church has withered in Europe,
Remained static in North America,
And exploded in Asia, Africa and
Latin America.
The church now has the goal to fulfill
Christ's command
To make disciples of all nations.
The long years of church history,
Brought salvation to many,
War and hatred to others.
The church is full of controversy.

SHERYE HANSON

Those who despair about the church
Must remember this,
The church is the body of Christ.
He chose us in spite of our imperfection.
To represent Him in the world.

Psalm 79 Your Holy People
By Sherye Hanson

O God, Europe imprisoned Your people the Jews.
Some protected them from the Nazis,
But most have handed them over to be put in prison camps,
Slaughtered and incinerated.
Every family has lost loved ones
Sometimes entire families were wiped out.
Yiddish is becoming a dead language.
Even though the United States could have given
Every Jewish person an American visa,
Our state department was too anti-semitic to do it.

Why did You allow such a horror to happen to them?
They are Your chosen people.
For what did You chose them?
Wrath?
The holocaust is over and gone.
Now there is a new nation Israel.
They have forgotten their suffering,
And have placed in on another people.
They bulldoze houses and prevent
Ordinary people from shopping for food.
They prevent Arabs from working to feed their families.
Their only crime is that they were on the land before the Jews.

God, why does one generation forget
The suffering of another.
Show them that the Arabs are people, too.
Open their eyes to the sin that they commit
Against their neighbors.
Christians do not see what is going on
They say that Israel is the innocent one.
But neither Jew nor Arab is without fault.
Both have committed crimes against each other.
Help Christian, Jew and Muslim see

That You alone are judge.
Bring peace again in Your Holy Land,
Prevent any more blood from being spilt.

Let them see that Jesus died for the sins of all.
He does not prefer one over the other.
He loves us all.
Open their eyes, Lord.
Open our eyes, Lord.
That we may see Your love is without partiality.
You love us all the same.

Psalm 80 Prayer for the Church
For Pastor Doug
And Living Hope
A Psalm of Love

Jesus, head of the body,
The church, Your bones, muscles and skin.
Needs Your resurrection life,
To be more than just a corpse
Churches in poor countries
Suffer poverty, persecution, and death,
Churches in rich countries
Experience decline, selfishness, and hypocrisy.
Come and save Your church.

Wake up the church in the rich world
Strengthen the church in the poor world.
Unite us together in hope,
That together we will be saved.

We have sinned against You, Jesus,
Instead of following You,
We have followed the world.
Instead of reaching out to sinners.
We have joined in their sin.

Great cathedrals are empty on Sundays,
Churches close and sell their buildings,
In China pastors are thrown in jail.
The Sudanese enslave Christians.

Wake up the church in the rich world
Strengthen the church in the poor world.
Unite us together in hope,
That together we will be saved.

You brought the gospel to Rome,
Pagans and Jews became Christians.
The blood of the martyrs planted the seed
And the Word spread throughout the Empire.

Then in time, all of Europe, then America
Followed by Asia and Africa
And the islands of the Pacific,
All came to know the name of Jesus.

In the very first churches,
Death and Decay have done their work.
Only a flicker here and there.
Most have fallen to the enemy.

Death and Decay in the rich Churches
Persecution and Death in the poor Churches.
Unite us together in hope.
That together we will be saved.

Psalm 81 Unfair Trade

To Christians
Who deserted me
For money and power

Joyfully sing to our powerful God;
Shout aloud to the Triune God!
Start the music, shake the tambourine,
Play the piano and saxophone.

Blow your trombone
And clarinet.
Shake those blues
With a Celebration Song.

God redeemed us.
Through His beloved Son
Whom He offered as a Sacrifice.
Because of His love for us.

He brought us out of a life of sin
Meaninglessness and despair,
Self-pity and anger
Was all we felt before.

We got caught and punished.
We cried for help
And You felt pity on us,
Gave us mercy instead of judgment.

We were like a restless crowd,
Disappointed and angry.
We forgot all about You –
Rioted in anger against You.

You called out with Your bullhorn
Come into my Assembly Hall

I have good news for you,
But we just threw more rocks.

"Once more I shouted and called to you.
But you ignored my pleas.
Instead you took my sacrifice
And crucified Him once again.

"You left Your first love
And worshipped money and power.
They have deserted you.
Now you are penniless and alone."

Psalm 82 Judgment for Judges
By Sherye

God chairs the great assembly
In the Supreme Court of Heaven.

How long, o Judges, will you defend the oppressors
And show partiality to the powerful?

Defend instead the cause of single parents
Stand up for the poor and oppressed.
Rescue the mentally ill, the disabled,
And the elderly from careless hands.

You judges are arrogant, ignorant and blind,
Without compassion, discernment and wisdom.
Justices who destroy justice.

You are like gods in your power.
But sinfully human in your ability.
You will die like those you judge.
Retire or lose your office like any official.

God, stand against these judges,
For the whole earth is under Your jurisdiction.

Psalm 83 Prayer for East Timor
A song of Sherye.

God, the world watches and does nothing.
While Indonesia attacks our people.
They do not want us to survive
As a nation and a people.
We have trusted in You all our lives,
Yet they burn our villages,
Kill our people
And steal our land.
Where are You, God?

Why does the world watch and not intervene?
Are they in league with the enemy?
Where are our brothers and sisters in Christ?
Are they paying attention?

They are more worried about Communists
Than they are about Christians.
They want to please Suharto
More than they want to act justly.

He and his army just decided,
That our side of the island should belong to them.
They invaded and took over,
Killing men, women and children.

Oh God, can't You overthrow his government.
Replace it with a different one –
One that will make peace
And remove their troops from our land.

Let him be like a puff of smoke,
A weed that the farmers burn.
Don't let him get away with it.
Open up the eyes of the world.

Let them see what he and his soldiers
Do to our people.
Wake up the church of God.
That they may pray for us.

Bring in a new government.
One that isn't interested in war.
Let the nations of the earth
Change the minds of the people.
So that we can live in peace.
No one governs without Your permission.
Please God, rescue us from him.

Psalm 84 For the Church

For the music director. An anthem for the choir.

Your home is in heaven,
But You have chosen to dwell in us.
The church, both visible and invisible,
Is Your home on earth.
We have built many beautiful buildings
As places to worship You.
From tiny rural churches
To great glorious cathedrals.

We know You don't live in churches,
But in the hearts of Christians.
You are the head of our body –
The foundation stone of our temple –
The beautiful community of Christ.

Our strength is not in numbers,
But our strength is in You.
We are walking together
On the journey of life.
Some can walk by themselves.
Others need someone to push them,
Or hold them by the hand.

We stop along the journey to rest
And listen to Your Word.
We drink the fresh pure water
From the Holy Spirit's well.

We pray along the journey,
Please help us to make it home.
Take care of us and love us
On this long and difficult road.

We look forward to living in Your house.
For we'd rather live with You.
Than to camp out with the sinners,
Who are sleeping by the road.

Although the journey is hard,
The cross is heavy
And we experience sorrow upon sorrow.
You provide for us all that we need.
Love and care for us each step of the way.
Keep us on the path towards home.
O great and powerful God,
It is good to trust in You.

Psalm 85 The Brick Church
For the music director. An anthem for the choir.

I was a wanderer, far from the Lord my God.
Sin was my favorite practice.
Lust my favorite emotion.
Then I got arrested
Stopped in my tracks.
Thrown into jail.
Without a friend in town.

I went to court,
Then served my time.
Working on the highway
In a chain gang.
I decided under the hot sun.
To get a new life.

The preacher came each Sunday
And told us to repent,
He was an old sinner himself.
When he was young, he stole cars,
Got drunk, and went to prison for a bar fight.
There he met God while reading the Bible.
For the next forty years
He came to the jail
And told his story to whoever would listen.

He got himself a job, carrying hod
Then learned how to lay bricks
Worked hard, got married, and had kids.
Every Sunday afternoon,
As faithful as a dog,
He would preach in jail.
Some would hear him.
Others would jeer him.
But he never stopped.

He built a congregation of men
Who'd been in jail.
He taught them to lay bricks,
And how to read God's Word.
Soon his congregation built
A colonial brick church,
Where they worshipped every Sunday.

He would tell them,
"Build your life on God.
He is the mortar that holds
Your bricks together.
Like love and faithfulness
Makes a marriage last.
So do truth and goodness
Make a life hold together.

I listened to his sermon.
When I got out of jail,
I went to the brick church
And learned to read God's Word.
I needed a job,
So first I carried hod
And then learned to lay bricks.
My life turned around.
Instead of a wanderer,
I built myself a house,
Married a wife,
And had a family.

Every Sunday afternoon,
I go to jail to tell my story.
The preacher's gotten too old to go.
I love that old man
With all of my heart.
I love God who saved me
And gave me a home
In a beautiful little brick church.

Psalm 86 Prayer for Sleep
Sherye's Prayer

Once again, Lord, I need Your help.
I try to do it by myself
But I can't.
Right now I'm tired and sick
And sick and tired of being so.
I haven't slept good for days,
I'm grouchy and just want to feel better.
Could You give me a good night's sleep
So that I can clean my house?

I know that You love me
No matter what I do.
I know that if I'm in serious trouble
I can call on You.
This isn't serious,
It's just annoying,
But please answer my prayer.

Among the powerful there is none like You.
No one has Your compassion
Someday all the nations
Will come and worship You.
They will recognize their Creator,
And come to give You honor.

For You alone are God,
Every other power is evil.
Only You do mighty and wonderful things.
For the benefit of all.

Teach me Your way of doing things.
Help me always to be honest and open.
I want a heart that is true
That I may always love You.

178

Thank You, God, for all You've done.
I will wait for my good night's sleep.
For You have helped me out
In situations worse than this.

I am depressed and feeling low.
Because of lack of sleep.
This is when the evil one comes.
And tells me You don't care.

He's a liar, I know for certain.
You are full of compassion, slow to get angry,
Overflowing with love and care.
I know that You will hear my prayer.
You will give me strength.

My enemy will see Your strength
And will back off and leave me be.
For he cannot confront You directly.
His power will soon be gone.
When You reign upon the earth.

Psalm 87 Jerusalem
An anthem for the choir.

Jerusalem, God's city,
Is a beautiful place.
Solomon at God's command
Built a temple on Mount Zion.
It is the city that all wish to visit
To pay homage to the Lord.
Yet it has known war and bloodshed.
Arabs and Israelis fight for it.
It is filled with sadness, for God's temple was destroyed.

God is building a new Jerusalem.
Large enough for all.
No one is excluded.
He invites everyone to live there.
If you accept His invitation,
This will be your eternal home.
God will write down your name
In His holy book.
In Jerusalem,
People from every nation, language and tribe.
Will sing together praises to God.
Praising God for the fountain of life.

Psalm 88 Complaint of an AIDS Patient
An anthem for the choir. Sung in a minor key. By Sherye Hanson

I am in so much trouble, Lord.
Please don't ignore me.
I am depressed and feel
Like I'm dead.
Why are You punishing me?
You have taken away my best friends.
They don't even want to see me.
They are tired of seeing me cry
And miss my laughter and jokes.

I pray to You every day,
Morning, noon and night.
Why are You letting me die –
In the grave I can no longer praise You.

What good can You do for me
After I'm dead?
Then it will be too late.
What is the point of letting me die?

I'll just rot and be gone.
No longer will You be able to help me.
Can Your love reach me in death?
Your miracles in hell?
Won't it be too late?
I've been sick and near death
For several years.
The doctors can't help me.
They just tell me I'm going to die
But they don't know when.
Death is my constant companion
My friends deserted me.
I no longer have a family –

They have left me here to die.
Where are You, God?

What benefit will You receive
If I die?
Please answer my prayer.
Heal me from this terrible disease.
Why do You reject me and hide Your face from me?

After I got HIV
I thought my life was over.
I did what I could but soon
I had full-blown AIDS.
I take all the medicine,
The way the doctor ordered,
But I've had pneumonia three times.
My lungs can't handle much more.

I'm so afraid, Lord,
I lie awake at night,
I think of all my friends
The ones I used to have.
I was a rising star in my chosen career.
I lost it all because of this disease.
Why can't You heal me?
I'm too young to die.
All I have left is my lonely
Hospice room.
Where are You, God?
I'm going to die!

Psalm 89 David's Dynasty

By Sherye Hanson

I will sing forever in the heavenly choir
With those saved by Jesus Christ.
We will sing of God's incredible love,
And His unbroken Word.

You made a promise to David,
That his throne would never end.
From Solomon to Zedekiah,
David's line was on the throne.

There is no one in heaven like You.
The heavenly angels who know You
Better than anyone,
Having been in Your service
For many generations.
Give You the highest praise.

There is none like You, God
In heaven and earth.

You rule over the stormy sea,
And still the unruly waves.
The ancient sea monsters are
As nothing to You.
Your strength conquers
All other powers.
You created heaven and earth,
And made them Your own.
The North and the South,
Arctic and Antarctica are Your creation.

Your character is based on goodness and fairness,
Love and consistency.
Those who know You and trust in You

Are very happy people.
They think of Your name all day long
And enjoy Your goodness.
You are their honor and strength.
Having You as their God just makes them look good
In the sight of all their neighbors.

We don't have a wimpy god,
Who sits upon a shelf.
We have the God of heroes.
You took a boy named David,
And gave him the strength of a man.
He killed a giant
Who made others quiver in fear.
You made him king of Israel,
The first of an eternal dynasty.
He conquered all the enemies that surrounded Israel.

Even though his sons didn't love God as he did,
God did not take the dynasty from him.
Fed up with the rebellion and rejection
From the kings of Israel,
Who preferred weak, useless idols
Over the Creator of heaven and earth,
God sent Babylon to conquer Judah.

Never again would a king be ruler over Judah.
Instead Babylon, then Persia,
Followed by Greece and finally Rome
Put their governors over the people of Judah.

The people of Judah returned to their land,
And rebuilt the temple.
But their hearts longed
For the restoration of the Kingdom of God
With David's son upon the throne.

O God, You did a wonderful and incredible thing.
You sent Your Son to be born of the line of David.
The eternal Davidic King.

Born in humility,
He died in disgrace on a Roman cross.
Despised and rejected by many,
He rose from death and ascended to heaven,
Where He reigns eternally.
No longer a kingdom of only Judah
But the King of all who believe in Him.
Praise the Lord forever!
Oh yes, Lord!

Psalm 90 Lincoln's Prayer

An imagined prayer by Abraham Lincoln
Based on the Gettysburg Address and the Second Inaugural Address

Lord God, since our country was founded
Four score and seven years ago,
We have worshipped You as our God.
Some of us came here on immigrant ships
Wanting to worship our own way,
Others came hoping for a better chance,
But Africans came on slave ships
In chains against their will.

You are the eternal God.
Before You formed the mountains,
Or filled the seas,
Planted trees,
Or placed animals on this earth,
You were there.

You made us out of dust,
And to dust we will return.
Like a flower that blooms
And soon wilts and dies,
We live briefly on this earth.

In this time in history,
You have chosen to punish us
For all the years in which we bought
And sold human beings.
The years in which we enslaved them,
Separated them from their families,
Whipped and chained them.

We are in the midst of a terrible,
Bloody, and long civil war.
State against state,

Brother against brother,
Many lives have been lost.
Men who should have been planting fields,
Building houses,
Practicing law
Are killing one another.

Finally, Lord,
We are beginning to see the end.
We have harvested the fruit of sin.
Now we will reunite as a broken people
With fear, hatred and resentments
In many hearts.

Teach us, Lord,
To love one another.
Let us use each moment we have
To build instead of tear down.

Let Your love satisfy
All our needs.
Then we can celebrate
And be glad for what time
We have left.

We must love instead of hate.
Then we can enjoy once again
Our unity as one nation under God
With liberty and justice for all.
Make our nation great –
Both in success and in goodness.
Bring justice to both black and white.
Repair the South that has suffered so much.

Enable the black man to support himself
By settling in the West on his own land.
You alone have the power
To make this great nation
Into a united, just and prosperous people.

Psalm 91 City Sanctuary

The one who lives in God's witness protection program,
Will live safe and secure.
I am one of them, "He has guarded me with His life.
I have complete faith in Him."

If Satan comes around
And tries to tempt me with sin,
God will protect me with His truth.
He is like a mother hen,
Who when the fox comes,
Gathers her chicks under her wings.
I won't be afraid of burglars, bombs,
Or things that bump in the night.
I will not worry about cancer or anthrax.

Many died in Oklahoma City,
Still more in New York.
But God has promised to protect me.
Even in terror events such as these.
Even if I die,
I will be in heaven with You.

If you live under God's protection,
Then you will never be harmed.
No national disasters will come to your house.
For He has an angelic army at His command,
To protect you day and night.
They will fly you out of there,
Before the enemy tries to trip you.

You will walk through darkened streets
In front of gangsters on the corner.
They will look but not touch
For God is always with you.

"Because he loves me," the Lord says,
"I will rescue him.
I will protect him, for he honors my name.
He will give a shout and I will answer.
I will be with him in temptation,
I will keep him from caving in.
He will live a long life pleasing to me
Until he goes up to glory."

Psalm 92 Sabbath

For Rest. By Sherye Hanson

Even when I feel tired and my back aches,
It is good to go to church and praise the Lord.
This morning I woke up at four
To pick up my friend,
Who was released from jail.
The streets were empty
Then I turned onto the street
Where we were supposed to meet.
There he was with his duffle
Sitting on the sidewalk.
He did not go to church today.
Instead he stayed home working.
I was sad that he couldn't see
That You wanted to see his face in church.

Work is good because You created us
In Your image to want to produce as You do.
The whole earth is alive with work.
Photosynthesis, chemical interactions,
Birth, growth and even decay.

We need our sabbaths to rest,
Rejoice and reflect.
Worship is our rest.
You created the world in six days.
On the seventh day You rested.
You also built in us a seven-day week.
Our bodies and minds need rest
Every seven days.

Foolish people try to work seven days
Without giving themselves rest.
They work their employees just as hard.

Then they wonder why mistakes are made.
Lives are lost because of defective products.

Those who listen to Your ways.
Who mix rest with work
Pleasure with pain
Don't fall into the workaholic trap.
They are like the bear
That hibernates in the winter.
The deciduous tree
That loses all its leaves in the fall.
There is a season and a time
For everyone and everything.
That is why You created
The Seventh day Rest.

Psalm 93 The Tides

The Lord our majesty set up His throne
Long ago before the world was made.
Then created the world
And set it firmly in its place.

God is our foundation when life's storms come in
He is our rock.
The wind and waves pound against the beach,
We are not moved.
Disease, death and destruction push us to our limit.
We are not moved.
Planted firmly in Christ, we hold fast against the waves.

The breakers roll in and the tide ebbs and flows.
You are greater.
The Spirit brings in waves of joy, persecution rolls out waves of pain.
We stand firm on the rock.
No matter how hard the waves and the wind push upon it.
The rock remains.

Psalm 94 Pay Back Time

Some argue that God is a God of love,
That He never will punish the wicked.
What kind of love is that, I ask,
For murderers, rapists and molesters
To get off without punishment?

Wicked men and women live upon the earth.
Many suffer no harm while they hurt others,
Yet they cause untold suffering to the poor and oppressed.
Will they get away with their crimes?

We make penniless murderers pay for their crime,
While corporate executives, slumlords and dictators die happily.
Some have stolen from widows and orphans,
Others have polluted the earth.
All have exploited the poor.

They have done their crimes in secret
Before people who refuse to see.
God is not blind to the crimes
They have done.
He hears their victims' cries.

God disciplines the man
And woman he loves,
Those who call God their master.
You protect them and guide them,
Throughout their whole lives
You will not give up on them.

God judges according to His own character,
Which is defined by love and truth.
He has mercy on those
Who repent of their sins.
And do God's will.

You rescue us from both sin and danger
If we call upon You.

Psalm 95 Listen

Come with me and sing a song,
To the Lord, our Cornerstone.
Give thanks with me for all He's done,
And praise Him with instruments and voice.

For our God is the great God,
King of kings and Lord of lords,
He holds the earth in His hands
And forms the mountains with His fingers.
He filled the oceans,
And built up the land to let it dry.

Come with me and bow before Him.
Kneel down and worship Him.
He is our Maker and Friend,
He is our Pastor and we are His people.
Listen to His words.

He spoke and there was light;
Is it too much to listen to His voice?
Don't become stubborn and refuse to hear.
For when our parents refused to listen,
They got divorced and we suffered.
They spent their money on booze instead of diapers.
We went to foster care instead of college,
All because they didn't obey.

Don't be like your parents.
Listen to God.
Stay out of trouble
Go to church.
Finish school and get a job.
Our parents lost out but should we have to lose, too?
We only need to hear God's voice.

Psalm 96 God's World

I will sing to the Lord a new song,
Wherever the nations meet.
At the United Nations, the Olympic Games and the World Cup.
I will take every chance that I get to tell of His love for the world.

The Lord is great
He is the only one always
Deserving of praise
He is the only true God,
The God who made the heavens.
Beauty, power and glory
Reveal to us His presence.

Nations of every continent,
Worship the Lord our God.
Honor His holy name.
Worship only Him
Come into His presence
And bring sacrifices to Him.

I will say to the United Nations,
"The Lord rules over the world.
He made it and it is beyond our control.
He will fairly judge each tribe and nation."

The heavens, the earth and the sea,
Sing to the glory of God.
The fields and forests dance His rhythm.
They will rejoice
And be happy to see
God's new creation
For now all creation cries out
From the curse of sin.
When Christ returns,
All creation will rejoice

In the salvation of our planet.
He will bring truth and healing
To all things on the earth.

Psalm 97 Worship the Creator

There is only one God,
Who rules the earth and skies.
Even when He hides from us,
He is always there.
He speaks with thunder
Fire and smoke pour our of mountains
At His command.
We see and hear the awesome power of our Creator.
Though His creation.

Some who see these marvels
Worship them instead of God.
Others create idols to obey.
They are empty images.
They have no power.
Power resides only in God.

Your people rejoice –
Those who worship You
In tiny churches, megachurches
And every size in between.
For You are the God of all the earth.
You are greater than any god.

We will love You above all.
We will hate evil
For You guard our lives
And deliver us from harm.
Your light will shine
Wherever we go.
We will be full of joy
And praise for our wonderful God,
Whose love is greater
Than anyone's love
And His goodness fills the earth.

Psalm 98 For A Cleaning Lady
A psalm.

I'm singin' to the Lord a new song.
The old song got tired and worn.
Instead of the blues I'm singin' allelues
'Cause God worked a miracle in my life.

I was stuck behind a broom and mop,
Scrubbin' floors all day
For people who just tracked in the mud
And talked behind my back.

I kept on scrubbin' and savin'
Those nickels and dimes,
That my employers grudgin'ly paid.
Now my son is a doctor and my daughter a CEO.

So all you lazy good-for-nothin' sinners
Who sit on your behind and complain,
Just remember that God helps lift up those
Who help to lift up themselves.

Now I'm dancin' and singin';
Shoutin' glory and praises to God.
For He lifted me off of that grimy old floor.
Into my own home sweet home.

When my son grad-u-ated from college
And went on to medical school,
I spent my time on my knees a prayin'
While I was scrubbin' those floors.

God answered my prayers
And He answered one more
My daughter just called up today.

Sayin', "Mamma you'll never believe it.
I'm the chief executive officer."

So I'm singin' allelues; I hear earth sing it too,
The sea and the mountains are dancin'
'Cause God answers prayers
For a woman who scrubs floors.
Isn't He a great God? Hallelujah Amen.

Psalm 99 Our God

There is a power greater than all,
The nations big and small.
He sits in heaven,
And watches each one.
Nothing escapes His eye.
We honor and praise His power,
And worship His holy name.
He is God the Father, the Son and Holy Spirt
The Trinity, the three in one.

Jesus is our King,
He reigns at God's right hand.
He will judge the nations
When judgment time comes.
He is worthy of honor and glory.
For He is the Lamb of God
Who sacrificed His body
For the sins of the world.

He is our high priest.
He also is our prophet.
He leads us through life
Through the Holy Spirit.
He speaks through His Holy Word
Written down by His apostles and elders.

He created the church,
To be His body on earth.
Men and women from every nation
Are members of His body.
He has united Jew and Gentile
Through His sacrifice.

Worthy is the Lamb of God
Of all honor and praise.

For His sacrifice
Covers the sins of the whole world.
He alone is worthy of our praise.

Psalm 100 Thanksgiving
A psalm for giving thanks.

I'm gonna sing and shout
I'm gonna dance to the Lord.
I'm gonna clap my hands
I'm gonna praise the Lord.
I love goin' to church Sunday morning.
And sittin' in the front pew.
When the worship team sings.
I'm singin' with them
And forgettin' everyone else.
I'm together with my family.

Don't come to church with a sour face.
Leave all your tears behind.
Put on a smile and remember
All the good things God has given.
Remember His love
And don't forget what He's done.
For His people throughout history.

Psalm 101 Song of the Judge
By Sherye Hanson

I'm a judge for King County Superior Court.
I love my job very much.
For I get to sort out the criminals
From the innocent men and women.

I'm careful to obey the speed limit
And never drink and drive.
I always cross at the crosswalk
And never jaywalk across the street.

I don't take bribes from anyone.
Nor do I socialize with lawyers,
Prosecutors or police officers.
I try to be completely fair.

I hate those who exploit the poor.
And abhor those who drive drunk.
Liars and thieves I can't tolerate.
Officers who only stop blacks I can't stand.

My mother was a drunk,
My father went to prison.
I love the law with all my heart.
For it is full of reason.

I want to insure that no one drives drunk.
Those who use drugs will quit
I know that jail doesn't make them stop.
So I send them to treatment for as long as I can.

I've heard from the others that no one likes me.
They'd rather go to jail
Than to go into treatment and be on probation.
For as long as is legally possible.

But I know that jail time's a joke.
Fines will never be paid.
The only thing that ever works.
Is treatment and probation.

So call me the hanging judge.
Complain about me to the bar.
But the all voters love me.
Because I clean up the streets
And make it safe to drive.

Psalm 102 Prayer of a Drug Addict
When he pours out his complaint before God.

God, if there is a god.
I'm in trouble.
I need dope real bad.
I know it's probably
Against Your rules
To use drugs.
Without them I can't cope.

Every part of my body aches,
It hurts to walk,
My heart beats too slow,
I'm not hungry,
And when I eat, food tastes bad.

I'm so skinny
None of my pants stay up.
My skin is dry and flaky.
I'm tired so I go to bed,
But I cannot sleep.
If I sleep, I wake up
Screaming with nightmares.

I watch television all day,
But see and hear nothing.
I'm afraid to go outside,
Because I owe everyone money.
My phone's shut off,
And soon my electricity will be too.
There's a pile of bills on the floor.
I can't think, move or pray.

But as I lay on the living room coach
My eyes wandered over to the bookshelf.
There I saw grandmother's Bible,

I remembered as a child
When she read to me its stories.
She would read about the Shepherd who cared for His sheep.
My favorite was about David, who was just a boy
When he killed Goliath with a stone in a sling.
Then she'd read about heaven and its streets of gold
Where she said she'd meet Grandpa someday.

I got down on my knees and prayed,
Just like I did as a child.
Then I prayed a childish prayer.
I couldn't think of another.
So I just talked to God
Like I talked to my grandmother.

"God, I don't know if you will listen.
I've done everything wrong.
I started smoking cigarettes
And then it was the weed,
Someone turned me onto crack
And then I started meth.
I became a garbage mouth,
Trying everything.
Now I'm completely broke.
I have no way to buy,
I'm in trouble, Lord.
Can you forgive me?
Can you bring my life back?"

I stayed upon my knees and wept.
Until I felt the Spirit
Come into the room
And fill my body and my soul.
I dried my tears and went to bed
And slept just like a baby.
The next morning I got up
And turned myself into jail.
I went to all the Bible studies.
N.A. meetings, and church services,
That were held in jail.

As soon as I had served my time.
I found my grandmother's church.
They welcomed me with open arms
And helped me find a job.

At first it was very hard
I became so depressed,
I wanted to go out and use again,
But something held me back.

I kept on working and paying my bills.
Going to meetings, church and probation.
Then finally I was free.
My muscles were strong,
And my eyes were clear.
I knew that God had healed me.
He had given me back my life.

Psalm 103 Praise the Lord

By Sherye Hanson

Praise the Lord, Sherye,
From the secret places in your heart,
Praise His name.
Don't forget what He does for you.
He forgives your sins,
Heals your body,
And brings you out of despair into hope.
He loves you, accepts you and comforts you.
His generosity overflows your tiny cup
You are forever young through His strength.

God brings justice to those like you
Who are oppressed.

God's history demonstrates His love.
He brought Israel out of Egypt,
And strengthened Moses to lead them.
Even though you have failed God many times,
He has been patient with you.
All He wants for you is His best.
There is nothing He won't do for you.
He sent His son to die for your sins.
Your sins are all forgotten,
Washed away under the blood of Jesus.
He doesn't remember any of your sins,
So don't remind Him of them.

All He wants from you
Is your love and obedience.
Is that too hard?
His Spirit empowers you
To do His will.
How can you fail?

He knows how fragile you are
And how short a time you will live.
He has eternal plans for you,
Starting now.
He made promises to you,
Which He will never break.
He promises never to leave you.
His presence fills the room where you sit.

God's rule is in heaven,
Where His will is always done.
He has invaded earth
With His Holy Spirit

He is creating
A mighty army of Christians,
Who will soon fight against
The enemy of our souls,
The war is over,
But the enemy has not conceded.
God has given him
A short time to end his rule.
Then He will return in power.
Conquer and govern earth.

Praise the Lord, Sherye.
Praise the Lord.

Psalm 104 Creation Hymn

Praise the Lord,

You are a great God.
The universe You created is a wonderful place.
Physicists study it in awe.
It expands ever greater for billions of years.
With both light and darkness in it.
The earth is surrounded
With an atmosphere of many layers.
The moisture of the clouds
Provides the rain and snow
That the land needs.
The winds follow a certain path
Designated by the Lord.
He set the earth
On its course around the sun.
In the beginning
The earth was covered with water.
But at His command the waters
Were placed into the oceans.
Great mountains arose
And dry land appeared.
Now there was ocean and land.
Never again will water cover the earth.

Underground springs open up to the surface
And water the ravines.
In them the deer and the elk,
The goats and the sheep,
And wild donkeys quench their thirst.
Birds build their nests by the rivers.
They sing among the branches,
Warning the other birds
That this is their territory.
Underground streams in the mountains

Water the mountain and surrounding hills.
God has created a marvelous system
To water all of the land.

He grows grass for the cattle.
Grains that farmers can cultivate.
The farmers grow food for the rest of us.
Wine to make us feel good.
Oil to clean our faces,
Bread to feed our stomachs.

The trees the Lord planted
Have plenty of water.
The six-thousand-year-old Sequoias
Grew so tall and we are in awe of them.
The eagles make their nests
High in the trees.
The goats live on the high cliffs.
The crags are a refuge for coneys.

The moon marks the seasons.
The sun marks the days.
The night provides shelter
For the beasts of prey,
As they hunt during the night.
The sun rises and they go to sleep.
The farmers rise early and go to the fields.

You have done many things, o God.
The earth is made by Your wisdom.
The animals and plants on the land.
The sea full of fish and animals large and small.
Incredibly large, the whales and the squid
Find their home in the spacious sea.

All look to You
To give them their food
When they are hungry.
You supply and they eat

You give with generosity
And they are satisfied.

If You hide Your face,
They have nothing to eat,
So they die and return to dust.
When You send Your Spirit,
They are created
And You renew the earth.

As long as God maintains the earth.
It will flourish and grow.
O God, protect the earth
From the ravages of the human race.

Your power makes the earth quake
And the mountains smoke.

I will sing about You all my life.
I will praise You as long
As I have breath to sing.

May this meditation on creation
Please the Lord.

Praise the Lord,
Praise the Lord.
Amen.

Psalm 105 God Gave Us a Book

Give thanks to the Lord,
Call on Him. He's always there.
Tell everyone about Him.
Sing praises to His name.
Say His name with honor and respect.
Those who seek God will find Him.
He wants to know you because He loves you.

Remember all that He has done for us.
While we were still pagans
Worshipping other gods,
He sent a man named Adoniram Judson,
To tell us all about Him.
He was born the 9th August 1788,
In Malden, Massachusetts,
The son of a Congregational Minister.
At three he learned to read
At ten he could read and write Latin and Greek.
At sixteen he entered Brown's College
There influenced by a skeptical friend,
He rejected Christ.
After a year of teaching
And living the double life
Of hypocrite and skeptic,
He quit his job,
And went New York
To write plays.
Mistaken and disappointed,
He went to Pennsylvania,
To live with his uncle.
On his way he stopped in an inn,
Alone in a room
He slept next door to a dying man,
The next morning the man died,
The man was his friend, the skeptic.

Shaken, he returned home.
He investigated the gospel once more,
And found the answers he sought,
Enrolled as a student at Andover Theological Seminary
Then fully assured,
He dedicated himself to the Lord.
God called him to be a missionary.
He then read a book about Burma,
An Account of an Embassy to the Kingdom of Ava.
A group of classmates founded
The American Board, which supported
Congregational foreign missions
For over a century
After it was founded.

Money was always a problem,
So, they sent Adoniram to London.
A French privateer captured his ship
And the French placed him in a French prison.
He escaped and decided
To get support in the United States.

He fell in love, married
And on 19th February 1812, now 24,
Adoniram, his wife Nancy
And another missionary couple,
Samuel and Harriet Newell, sailed from
Salem, Massachusetts on board
The brig Caravan.
Their destination – India.

While sailing, he translated
The New Testament
Studying the Bible convinced him
That the Baptists were correct about baptism,
So in Serampore, India,
Adoniram and Nancy were baptized.
He resigned from the Congregationalists,
And became an American Baptist
Without support from a missionary society.

Dr. Carey told him that Burma
Was different from the book.
Burma sounded hopeless,
He couldn't stay in India,
So they planned to sail to Java.
The East India Company harassed them
So from Madras, they took the only boat,
That was bound for Rangoon in Burma!

The Judsons were often sick
And they suffered at the hands
Of corrupt Burmese officials.
They learned the language, printed tracts, and
portions of the New Testament.
Their first breakthrough came
When he built a Zayat,
a Buddhist-style meditation room
On a main street
Where he could hold meetings
And teach passersby.
This broke down barriers
Between him and his hearers,
Maung Nau believed in Christ,
Their first convert
After they worked in Burma 6 years.

The conversion of Maung Nau
"Gave the mission a new impetus":
Rangoon's idle curiosity
About the new religion had been satisfied.
Others sought to know Christ also.

Adoniram tried unsuccessfully
To petition the despotic Emperor
To allow religious freedom,
But he would not listen.
His rule brought more persecution
To the new believers.
But they did not falter.

Burma raided the East India Company land.
The Company fought back and war began.
Adoniram was thrown into death prison
With the other foreigners.
Nancy remained free and managed
To look after her husband,
Petition for his release,
And deliver and care for another child.
He was released
And Nancy died.
Judson became an interpreter.
Peace returned in 1826
Burma was more closed than ever.

After recovering from the loss of Nancy,
Judson continued
with his translation of the Burmese Bible.
At this time Ko Tha Byu,
A member of the Karen tribe, became a Christian.
The Karen believed that they would learn
About God through a lost book.
Many Karen became Christians.
Judson's translation of the Bible
Was that book.
Adoniram Judson died on 11th April 1850.
It was no accident that Judson read
A book about Burma.
It was God's answer our cry.
It was we, the Karen,
Who sought to find the lost book.
Which God supplied through Adoniram Judson.

Psalm 106 Two Nations

Praise the Lord.

Thank You, God, for Your incredible love for me.
You've been so good to me.
Who has the words to describe
What You have done?
Those who do justice
And always do what is right
Will always be happy.
You will not forget us
When You pass out the rewards.
I want to be part of the Kingdom of God,
And share in its wealth of love and mercy.

I am a member of two nations,
The Kingdom of God
And the Republic of the United States of America.
We Americans have sinned even as our ancestors.
We have killed and defeated the native peoples
And shut them up on worthless lands.
We have bought and sold Africans,
And made them into slaves.
Once freed, we beat them, lynched them
And put them into prison.

During World War II we refused
To give refuge to the Jews
Who were being slaughtered by the Germans.
We also put in camps, loyal Japanese
Americans whose only crime was their ethnicity.

Now we are determined that Arabs
And Muslims are our enemy.

We have hated many peoples, Lord.
Forgive us for our hatreds
And bring love into our hearts.
You loved us so much,
That You sent Your Son to die for us.
I hope that we are willing to die
For the sake of justice
To sacrifice our abundance
To those who are hungry.
To speak against injustice
No matter who does it.

Our nation has suffered through
Two world wars, a civil war,
And several other wars.
We have experienced drought,
Famine, and floods.

We have also prospered to become
The richest country on earth.
Make us to be the most generous
And give out of our wealth to those in need.

We ask You to change our hearts
So that the disgrace of homelessness
In the richest country on earth
Will be erased.

We pray that drug abuse
That has enslaved our children
And corrupted many Third World nations,
Will be eliminated.

We repent of our love of money.
Replace that love with love for You.
We must put people before things,
Justice before wealth.

You have done great things for us;
Given us victory in war;

Freedom of religion, speech;
The press, and unlawful arrest.
And many other freedoms.
We must use our freedom for love
Rather than for hate.

Remind us to be good stewards of the earth.
To not poison the soil, water and air
Of this land we share with the animals.
We need to protect their homes
From destruction and harm.

Fill our hearts with gratitude towards You.
Love for the people from every nation,
And respect for the land and its creatures.

Amen.

BOOK IV

Psalm 107 The Boarding House

Thank You, Lord, for the rooming house,
Where I lived pregnant and single,
With eight other women of various strengths
Who came from all over the country.

I was twenty-one when I moved into that house,
Alone, full of morning sickness and self-pity.
I lived on welfare and took care of my body,
And prepared to be a mother.
Most of the women were students,
We lived on University Hill,
One block from the shopping center,
One block from the campus.

Our manager, Jeannette,
Was one year older than me,
But so much more responsible.
She managed the house
And ministered to each one of us.

Another woman, Rachelle,
Who'd graduated from college
And worked on two different newspapers,
Was between careers.

Pam was engaged to be married
To a future seminary professor,
She was petite and from Texas.
Her wedding was very grand.

Nikki, also engaged,
Had traveled the world.
She visited Spain
And had lived in the Philippines.

Her wedding was in the chapel
With only a few guests.
We sang hymns
And ate wedding cake in the courtyard.

Wendy, shy like me
Worked in a nursing home.
Her parents were divorced.
She was learning about God.

Jackie was an athlete,
She became a Christian in college
Her desire was to be a disciple
And to learn at Jesus' feet.

Beverly had long dark hair
And an ivory complexion.
A beauty she would have been
If her teeth had been straightened.

While she lived at the house
She had a psychotic break.
And I saw a friend transformed
Into someone with delusions.

Rick, who became Reuben,
Was a frequent visitor.
He also became ill
And thought he was the Messiah.

Margie, a quiet Presbyterian
Wore braces on her teeth from the age of seven,
She had big brown eyes
And a sunny disposition.

There were others who moved in
When some of us moved out.
Nikki and Pam got married
Terri then moved in.

For me the house was the place
Where I first experienced
Grace, love and acceptance.
In spite of my critical nature

I learned how to cook.
And how to be a hostess.
It requires a laid-back attitude
And a warm friendliness.

Jeannette would hold house meetings
And talk about I Peter,
I never really understood
Why she loved that letter.

She vaguely referred
To abuse she had experienced
At the hand of her father.
Who stole her innocence.

She was searching for a witness,
Who would back up her story
And hold her Dad accountable
For the crime that he had done.

Merry came after I left,
When she had to be restrained
Else she'd throw herself out the window.
Jeannette restrained her with a hug and quiet words.

They moved to a bigger house.
There they created a hospice for Patience
Who was dying of cancer.
Before that, only her twin, Prudence, cared for her.

Then they moved across country
To an old, fallen-apart mansion.
Where they continued their work
For the troubled and dying.

Darla, a woman with serious diabetes
Whose husband left her
Lived under their care
Until she died.

They provided shelter for the mentally ill,
The old and the dying.
Jeannette, whose father killed her desire to marry,
Became a mother to children
Whose parents were too ill to care for them.

She worked out her guilt for what her father had done,
Through caring for the ones no one else loved.
God brought us into that house
Some for a short time.
Others for a lifetime.
There we experienced mercy,
Forgiveness and love.
Now they call themselves
The 107th Psalm Christian Family.
God bless their home, and each member.
Make them prosper and continue.
A place of healing
For women like me.

Psalm 108 Ministry

A song. By Sherye Hanson

My love for You never stops,
That is why I want to sing.
Bring out the guitar,
The fiddle and the banjo.
Wake up the crowd.

I'm going on tour, Lord,
To every place on earth.
I want everyone to hear
All about Your wonderful love.

Your love is so great
That it reaches the most distant star.
You are as faithful as the sky is high.
I want to write Your name on the clouds,
And broadcast to the whole earth
The glory of Your presence.

Help me, Lord, with all Your strength,
Save the one who loves You.
I hear His voice from heaven,
"Don't worry about your debts,
or the mortgage on your house.
You don't need to look at your bank statement.
Or figure out how much you owe.
Don't sell your car and your furniture.
I know that things have been hard.
I will save your house.
I won't take away your car,
I'll make sure your debts are paid."

"But God," I protest, "if it wasn't for You
Forgetting about me,
I'd have my debts paid

And my mortgage payments would be on time."
But then I recalled all the days of my ministry,
That I'd never gone hungry or lost my house.
He'd always provided enough.
I don't have to worry about the bank.
He'll take care of it all.

Psalm 109 Forgiveness and Not Revenge
For the music director. By Sherye Hanson.

When I quit my job as a pastor.
I was accused of many things.
Some of them were true.
Some of them were false.
Most of them were distorted.

I felt completely betrayed,
But also guilty.
I shut the door to reentry
Into the vocation for which I was called.

Only two friends from the church continued to see me.
Others thought it was wrong to have contact with me.
I was a pariah in the church.
No one understood what had
Happened to us.
No one listened to our story.
There was no one who cared
About our family.
We were left on our own.

But God cared.
He sent a missionary family
Who met us the first Sunday
In the new church to which we went.

God in His wisdom.
Told me to go.
I felt alone
But I was not.
God had not left me.

The church has gone in a different direction.
From the direction in which I am called.

For my calling isn't to the righteous.
Who come to church for themselves.
My call is for the needy and oppressed.
Who know nothing of God's love.

I have forgiven that pastor.
I have even forgiven myself.
God has brought good things from this.

I am no longer tempted to become ordained.
I will always be just one of the laity.
My role will be at the door of the church.
Inviting those in who feel
Uncomfortable in church.
Making room for them in God's house.

Thank You, God, for my enemy.
May he do well and succeed.
Bless him and the church that I left.
Bless me also in my ministry.
At the door of the church.

You have been good to me.
Even though I lost the place I held.
For You are the one who orders my steps.
My work is to follow and obey.
Amen.

Psalm 110 Our Warrior Priest
By Sherye Hanson

Our Lord, the priest, like Melchizadek,
Will reign upon the earth.
He will build His throne in Jerusalem

And rule over all the earth.
His rule will be as new as the dawn in the morning.
A fresh beginning for this tired old earth.

When He comes, all nations will go against Him.
They will be defeated
And their bodies will be piled in heaps.
Their rulers will be judged and punished.

He will come.
Don't forget.
God's promise to Him
Will not be changed.

O Come Lord Jesus.

Psalm 111 God's Law
Praise the Lord

I will honor the Lord with all my heart
In the legislature and rules committee.
God's works surpass anything we can do.
All who examine them are delighted.

He brings order to the universe,
His laws order everything
From the tiny atom
To the largest star.

He operates with elegance and generosity.
His economics provides more than enough for all.
Our economics means inequality and starvation.
We operate with incompetence and greed.

Our God demonstrates His power
Over all nations on the earth.
We may have the biggest army,
But He determines the victor.

We may dispute our borders
But He determines the size of them.
Our laws have unintended consequences.
His are perfect in every way.

We would be wise to use His laws
As a guide to writing our own.
Beginners who follow Him
Are soon wiser than independent elders.

Psalm 112 Honor God
Praise the Lord.

The one who honors the Lord,
Who delights to do His will
Is the happiest man or woman
Upon this wonderful earth.

Her children will be well-known
His sons will follow the Lord.
She will have plenty of money.
He will own a substantial stock portfolio.
Even in the hard times
They will survive.
The kind and caring family
Will be successful in what they do.
Their generosity will be well paid.
He will always be remembered.
She won't worry about bad news.
His heart will trust the Lord.
She will be secure.
When life is over, he will triumph.
She gives her time and her gifts to the poor.
His goodness will last forever.
They will name hospitals after her.

The one who has his own way
Will be angry with those
Who honor God.
Her desires will come to nothing.
His will vanish like fog in the sun.

Psalm 113 For God's Workers
Praise the Lord

Workers of the Lord
Unite to praise the Lord.
Today and forever,
From the East to the West,
Morning until Night,
Praise His name.

The Lord rules over the nations
And He reigns over the heavens.
Who is like our God, more powerful than all,
Yet in kindness he reaches down to oversee
Each detail of heaven and earth.

The day laborer sitting by the road,
Waiting for a job,
He hires to work for himself
The King of kings.
The barren mother gives birth
to many new children of God,
Raising them to be disciples.

Praise the Lord.

Psalm 114 Immigrant Church

When my family left Sweden,
To worship the Lord with enthusiasm.
Kansas became a sanctuary.
Minnesota God's country.

They traveled on ships,
These seasick farmers.
Then they traveled by train
To the prairies.

They founded a Swedish church
In the middle of the country in Kansas
They named it the Brantford Mission Covenant Church.

They first had services in Swedish,
Then they had them in English.
It was a small church that
Grew as more people came
From miles around.
To worship the Lord God there.

In that church my father worshipped.
My grandparents celebrated in that church
Sixty years of marriage.
It is not a monument,
This historic church,
It is alive and growing
With the Spirit of God.

Psalm 115 God Gets the Credit

We may have done difficult things,
But the credit does not go to us,
The credit goes to God.

Others put their trust in money,
Stocks and bonds, and bank vaults.
Some are secure behind ten locks
On their apartment door.
Many find security is having
Good insurance.

We may have all of those,
But they are not God,
They cannot provide.
Only God can help us through.

Some go to support groups,
Small church groups
Or depend on family support,
We do too.
But they are not good enough.
They cannot comfort.
God is the only one our family can trust in.

God, help us to always trust in You.
You are the one who helps us
When things get hard.
God remind us to depend on You.
And not just on our friends.
You are always faithful
And never too busy.

The Lord remembers us.
He prays for us every day.
Sitting at the right ear of the Father,

Jesus whispers to Him all our needs.
He will give us our heart's deep desire,
Love us with eternal love,
And provide peace during the hard times.
He is our God.

God will expand our ministry.
Our family will shine with God's love.

Heaven belongs to the Lord,
But earth belongs to humanity.

We will praise the Lord while we live.
Those who have died are no longer heard.
We must bring honor to God now.

Psalm 116 New Life

I will always love You.
When I cry out to You for mercy,
You hear me and respond to my need.

Death had called my name.
I was lying in a hospital bed
In intensive care.
I was breathing though a ventilator.
Unconscious and barely alive.

I heard the doctors and nurses say,
"This one is a goner.
I've never seen anyone this sick
Survive the night."

I could barely think.
My brain was full of cotton.
But I said, "Oh God,
This is a bad time to die.
My children are young,
My husband can't cope.
I need to come out of this fog.
Please, Lord, bring me back."

That night I struggled to breathe
My fever burned me up.
Then in the morning my fever broke,
I fell into deep, restful sleep.
In the evening when my husband came.
To visit me at my bed.
I opened my eyes, smiled and said,
"Guess what, I am still alive."

My husband said, "Thank God,
I prayed all night for you."

He kissed me with tears in my eyes.
I took the ventilator off,
Because I could speak and breathe on my own.
Then I got out of bed and gave him a hug.
All the alarms went off.
The nurses all flew into my room.
They saw me standing
And stood there in shock.
I was alive.

They shooed me back into bed.
And called my doctor up.
He came from his dinner to see.
His patient who had survived

He examined me
And checked out the statistics
From all of the machines.
Then said, "I think she's well.
Let's keep her overnight in the med. unit,
And if she's the same we'll release her.
Get all her blood work done Stat."

The next day, the doctor declared me well.
And sent me home that day.
"I don't understand it
But I think you'd call it a miracle."

I went home
And took care of my children and spouse.
I praise You and thank You, my God.
How can I ever repay You, o Lord?
I can't, You know I'll always owe You
For my life and health.
I will live each day for You.
Full of gratitude.

Psalm 117 Praise the Lord

Praise the Lord,
Everybody
Praise the Lord
Every nation
Praise the Lord
Every tribe.
For God is good
And His love never ends.

Praise the Lord.
Oh yes, Lord.

Psalm 118 Hosanna, God Saves Us

I stood in front of the congregation.
To tell them what God has done for me.

"Give thanks to the Lord with me
For He is good and His love lasts forever."
Then the congregation stands
And we say together,
"His love never ends."
The pastor then says,
"His love goes on forever."
The choir echoes with song,
"His love is eternal."

"I want to tell You about how God rescued me.
I was full of anger and anxiety.
I felt that my parents never loved me.
Nothing I did was right.
Only my brothers were loved."

"I never knew what love was.
I grew up and left home.
Got a job and lived alone.
I did well but had no friends.

Then the loneliness got to me.
One day I couldn't get out of bed.
I called in sick for a week.
Then finally I called the doctor.
Who sent an ambulance.

I didn't stop crying for hours.
I couldn't say a word.
I was so sad and so alone
I couldn't deal with it.

The doctor gave me pills.
I went to group therapy.
Nothing changed my mind.
I just felt self-pity.

One night an angel came
And stood at the end of my bed.
Dressed just like a nurse,
I thought she'd come to take my pulse.

She said, "I'm a messenger from God.
He has heard your cries.
And wants you to know
How much He truly loves you."

"What am I to do?" I said.
I feel so all alone.
I cannot feel anything but sad.
How can I know about God?"

She told me to get up
And put on my street clothes,
To fix my face and hair.
I was going to be released.

I followed her out of the room.
And signed the paperwork.

"Go to the nearest church
And open up the door.
Put in some coins
And light all the candles.

"Then remember all the ones
Who no one liked to sit with.
The boy in a wheelchair.
And the girl with C.P.

"Those are the ones with whom.
I will build my church.

Those who the world has rejected.
Will be the cornerstone."

I looked up at my old classmates
And brought them all to church.
You are sitting here now,
Listening to my story.

Then one by one they came
To one of the altars
And lit a candle.
Till every one was lit.

Then I gave them all a branch
And we walked around the church.
Shouting "Hosanna,
God save us."

We carried a banner that read,
"Give thanks to the Lord.
His love lasts forever."

Psalm 119 God's Guidebook

<u>ˋ Aleph</u>
A day that starts with reading the Bible,
Always puts the focus in the right place.
Attitude doesn't come from external events.
Attitude comes from a focused heart.
Anyone can have a bad day.
All you have to do is focus on what's wrong.
All God's people can have a good day,
Alert to the actions of God.
Average people focus on events,
Aware only of what they can see.
Alone in the world, without God's help.
Amplifying all their problems.
Acting on their impulses, ignoring God's Word.
Alert people see God in all the wonders of the world.

<u>b Beth</u>
Before you can mature and become an adult,
Blameless living is difficult.
Butted on all sides by temptations,
Better young adults than you or I have fallen.
Begin your youth by putting God's Word in your heart.
Believe in Him when things get rough.
Build your life on things of heaven.
Blame only yourself when you fall into sin.
Bring every sin to Jesus and repent.
Begin anew with prayer and meditation.
Boldly come into His presence.
Bad influences will bring you to ruin.
Break off those relationships.
Battle temptation by avoiding it.
Borrow wisdom from those who have it.
Bow before the truth of God.

g Gimel

Give God the glory for His gifts to you.
Gain only Jesus and lose the world.
Great things are intended for us.
Green cards in this world is all we have.
Goals are for heaven, not for this earth.
Go for the goal of knowing Him.
Greet each day by learning and living the Word.
Gone are yesterdays, we only have today.
Give all you can to the poor and the Lord.
God will provide for your needs.
Guidance comes from those who obey.
Grin at your enemies and greet them hello.
God will repay them for all that they've done.
Gaze every day into His dear face.
Gone will be the tears and sorrow,
God's love will wipe them away.

d Daleth

Done is the word we all want to hear.
Delighted to know that our hard work is complete.
Do unto others as you would want them to do to you.
Dare to be obedient to God's commands.
Diligently work to understand His will.
Deal with your difficulties by giving them to God.
Draw on His strength for He wants you to
Depend on Him every day.
Deceit and lies are not God's way.
Decide to follow Him through every storm.
Don't let the devil stand in your way.
Dedicate your heart and your life to God
Detest evil and don't deny it exists.

h He

He alone is God.
Heaven obeys His every word.
Hell rebels against Him.
Hear His Word and listen.
Hand over your life to His Word.
Hurry to obey His commands.

Happiness will be your daily reward.
Health and a good life will come.
Hearing God's Word and doing it,
He, the Lord God rewards.
Help me, Lord, to comprehend
How high, wide and broad is the Law.
Head me in the right direction.
Happiness is found in going Your way.
Hand in hand we'll go together,
Having a relationship not based on wealth.
Hating the evil and loving the good,
Healing my heart of its brokenness,
Healer of my Soul You'll be.
Heaven waits me –
Home to be with You.
How I long to be in Your presence –
Hindered not from doing Your will,
Honed through suffering into perfection,
Held for eternity.

w Waw
Wonderful God, I am in awe of You.
Write on my heart Your will.
Willful I am and often I
Wander away from You.
When someone criticizes me,
Wipe away my tears.
Win the battle in my heart,
Which wishes to retaliate.
Weld Your words upon my mind
Which You want me to remember.
Wake my heart to love my enemy.
Wicked though he might be.
Willing I want to be to speak.
Wise words written in Your law.
Wisdom only comes from You.
Wickedness from me.
Wash away my sin and doubt.
Wreath me with Your kindness.
Where You lead me I will then follow,

Wrapped up tightly with Your love,
Wondering why I trust You now,
Willing to do Your will.

z Zayin
Zealously I will love Your law.
Zest for life will be the result.
Zigzags will be gone from my path.
Zero will be my falls.

th Heth
There are many who fall away.
They do not keep on the path.
Thinking a shortcut will get there faster.
They fall and disappear.
That way is the way to getting lost.
This road will lead us home.
Their ways are not Your ways.
Though I rebelled and left You.
There never was a day You left me.
Thankful again for Your guidance.

y Yodh
You are my heart's desire.
Young or old are loved by You.
Yes is Your favorite word.
You love to give good gifts to
Your children on earth.
Yet sometimes we need to hear no.
You set the boundaries for us.
Your boundaries are clear and right.

T Teth
Every day I need to read Your Word.
Even when I'm busy or tired.
Else I will slip and fall.
Everyone must listen to Your commands.
Elevate the Word to its proper place.
Eternal God and eternal Word.

Excellent and Holy God –
Explain Your Word to us.

k Kaph
King of kings You are.
Kindly and tenderly You rule
Keeping both animals and humans.
Kinship You offer us through Jesus Christ.
Killed upon a criminal's cross.
Kyrie eleison

l Lamedh
Love is the secret in Your Word.
Life is what we receive when we
Live it.
Laughter comes from children.
Labor from their fathers.
Lighten our load,
Lord.
Lift up our head so that we can see You.
Long are the heavy days of work.
Lead us to Your place of rest.
Leaning on You and
Letting go of all that troubles us.

m Mem
Memorize the Word, my child.
Memories are better when you're young.
Make each moment count for God.
Music is part of worship.
Mindfulness is our response.
Meditate on God's Word every day.
Meet Him early in the morning.

n Nun
Never go to bed angry,
Nothing will hurt your sleep more.
Nothing is worth a grudge.
Needy and humble go to God.
Kneel before Him.

No prayer is unheard by God
Note down every word he says.
Knowledge of His Word
Numbers us among the blessed.

s Samekh
Sustain me by the Word.
Save me from myself.
Self-centered to the core.
Seeking only what pleases me.
Center me in Your will.
Seek me when I stray.
Scalp to heel, let me feel
Saved, delivered, healed.
Seeking only to please You, Lord.

v Ayin
I look for help from Your Word.
Instructions for living are in Your law.
In You alone I trust.
Instinct and intuition aren't enough.
I need the law to guide me.
I am Lord of all the earth.
In Him all things are held together.
Invite me to Your table.
Insight and wisdom You give us.

p Pe
Praise You, Lord, for giving us Your law.
Put your trust in Him.
People perish without a vision.
Provide us with a goal in mind.
Proven through adversity.
Purify my mind and heart.
Push us and pull us
Place us where You want us to be.
Prayer and scripture are the key.
Putting You first above all things.
Panic not, the Lord is near.
Peace He gives us through His Word.

People who obey the Word.
Please You above those who just read it.

c Tsadhe
Cease to fear, O restless heart.
Center your life in Him.
Celebrate by prayer and Word.
Cycle prayer, praise, and law.

q Qoph
Quiz me on my knowledge of You.
Quiet my heart that worries.
Quench my thirst for You.
Qualify me for the Kingdom.

r Resh
Release me from my guilt and shame.
Render me soft and gentle.
Read to me from Your law.
Reality is defined by You.
Revive my Spirit,
Rock upon whom I can depend.
Roaring waves may frighten me.
Rolling over me.
Rescue me from the turbulent sea.
Reveal to me Your powerful hand.
Resting in my Father's arms.

S Sin and Shin
Seven times a day is not too much to
Seek Your Heart and Will.
Sinners hate Your Law.
Saints love to follow it.
Some try and fail.
Sitting on the fence.
Seeking to have it both ways
Sin and salvation.
Save me from my stupidity.
Set my face in Your direction.

Send me to teach sinners Your way.
So that they will not suffer in hell.

T Tau
To You alone I call for help.
Take my hand and lead me home.
Teach me Your ways, o Lord,
Trip-ups I don't need.
Tenderly You show me where I'm wrong.
Tune my heart with Your laws.
Terrible things can happen when I
Take the wrong road.
Tempted by the pleasures of sin,
Tasting of the lust of evil.
Trusting not in Your ways but only my own.
Trouble follows when I disobey Your law.
Trust in God and You will never fall.

SONGS FOR THE PILGRIMS

CLIMBING THE MOUNTAIN
TO WORSHIP GOD

Psalm 120 For A Psychiatric Patient
Climbing Song

Whenever I'm scared, anxious or depressed.
I call on the Lord and He answers me.
Save me from lies and liars.
Won't He punish those who lie,
With sharp knives and hot coals?

God, I hate staying in the hospital,
With nurses and doctors who lie.
They only cause trouble.
I am a woman of my word.
All they want is war.

If I say I won't take the medicine
Because it's poisoning me.
They tell me I'm just paranoid
And tell me to go home.
If I take the medicine,
My chest hurts, shooting knives
Go up my legs.
What am I to do, Lord?
Why do they want to kill me?
I am a woman of peace.

Psalm 121 My Hiding Place
A climbing song.

When I climb up Mount Zion to Jerusalem
To worship the Lord,
I think of the times when I've needed help
To escape all my problems.

Some look to the mountains to hide
From their enemies,
But I know that God will protect me
Wherever I may go.

So instead of running to the mountains.
I run into my closet.
Pray to God for help
And to watch out for me.

God never sleeps,
He never stops watching
God never leaves me.
And He never fails.

So why should I run to the mountains?
I run into His arms, where I am always safe.

Psalm 122 On Holiday
A climbing song.

I love to go on holiday to worship the Lord.
We all go together up the Mountain of God.
We leave early the day before.
Carrying food and blankets.

The road is long, hard and steep up the mountain.
But it is so much fun to travel with our families.
Sometimes my daddy carries me upon his shoulders.
When it gets dark and my feet get tired.

Dad lays our blankets down next to the road.
Mom passes us bread, cheese, raisins and water.
Then exhausted we lie down.
And Dad covers us up with a blanket.

We wake up early in the morning.
And travel like we did before,
But the road is steep and we are tired
And we no longer sing.

Then we come to the gates of the city.
Which is covered with flowers and branches.
There are flags for each of the tribes.
And banners proclaiming God's love.

We come to the court of the temple.
Where thousands of people are.
We greet one another with Shalom, shalom.
We sing and shout to the Lord.

The King delivers to each one of us.
Bread, raisins and honey.
Water comes from the spring.
And tastes as pure as sunshine.

Then on the way home from our holiday.
Dad tells us that every day we must pray.
For the city of cities, the city of God.
That peace may always be there.
That the temple will prosper
And we will be healthy for the next holiday.

Psalm 123 Bullies

A climbing song.

I look up to You, my God,
You are my Savior,
Just as employees look to their bosses,
Girlfriends look to their boyfriends,
Husbands look to their wives –
We look to You for help.

We have been through a lot, God,
Our enemies jeer at us,
They yell curses to shame us
In front of our neighbors.
Lord, please help us.

Psalm 124 For Parents

A climbing song. Of Sherye.

If God was not by our side,
Let's say it together
If God was not by our side,
When our daughters became ill.
We couldn't have dealt with it.
The pain would have crushed us.
Sorrow would have filled our hearts.
We wouldn't have been able to love them
And be with them until they got well.
The pain would have been too much.

Praise the Lord that He's given us strength.
To handle mania, psychosis and depression.
And deal with doctors, emergency rooms and insurance companies.
Once more we weathered the storm.
We've gotten through another episode.
Britta is better than ever.
Kurt and I love each other more.
Nathan and Kristina still trust in You.
Your name is the one we call.
The Creator of heaven and earth.

Psalm 125 Trust in God
A climbing song.

Those who trust in God
Are like Mount Everest,
Which cannot be blown away.
God surrounds His people,
Like the mountains surround Tibet.
He protects His people from all directions.

Though Satan's rule is on the earth.
It will not remain forever.
He has been defeated at the cross.
At the last battle,
When Christ returns.
His rule over earth will be broken.

Lord, protect Your children until then,
Through wars, earthquakes and storms.
Turn the hearts of those
Who don't yet love You.
Bring in the last person who is lost.
Bring peace to the world.

Psalm 126 Sweet Good-bye
A climbing song

When Janaee and Scott return,
To live in our house,
We will be full of joy.
To send them away
Was difficult for us.
We loved their presence so much.
But they didn't listen,
They didn't hear.
For them it was a day-by-day existence.
They had no goals or plans.

God has great plans for us.
He paid a very high price for humanity.
Our lives are worth more than the wealth of empires.

We sent them away with tears.
We will welcome the home with hugs and gifts.
They went out weeping,
Carrying the seed of God in their hearts.
They will return,
Carrying in the harvest.

Psalm 127 A Christian Family
A climbing song. By Sherye Hanson.

Unless God establishes your family,
It will not last.
Unless God guards your marriage,
It will end in divorce.
You can work hard and love each other,
You can scrimp and save and do everything right.
But it will come to nothing unless God does it.

On the other hand, if you give your family to Him,
Your children will be a gift from God.
They will honor His name and yours.
So sinner, repent of your sins,
Put your family in God's hands.
And your family will be safe in Him.

Psalm 128 Happy families.

A climbing song.

Happy families are all alike,
They serve and honor God.
They work hard and yet take time to play.
The wife has many children,
The children grow up healthy,
That is what we expect from the Lord.

Yet sometimes God gives sick children to good parents.
And healthy ones to careless parents.
Wives and husbands die young.
In other families children never come.
Is this because God punishes the good
And rewards those who do wrong?

Though God gives good gifts to his children.
He also gives us pain.
We suffer just as Jesus does
And our inheritance comes
When we go to heaven.

We have the peace
That is beyond human understanding.
God is always with us
Through hurt, sorrow and pain.

Psalm 129 For a slave
A climbing song. By Sherye Hanson.

My name means worthless.
That's what they called me all my life.
My parents sold me to a farmer
So that I could separate
The tiny rice plants from each other
With the tiny fingers of my tiny hands.

He used me and abused me.
Then war came.
I was caught between armies.
And fled across the great river.

There I lived in camps
Until a sponsor came
I went to live in the basement
Of a Christian's house.

When I knew just Buddha,
I experienced only shame.
But then I learned about Jesus,
No longer am I worthless,
I have a new life.
I'm married with children.
And have God in my heart.

Psalm 130 Come Home
A climbing song.

When I am most afraid,
I call on You.
Please, God, listen to me.
I need mercy right now.

I need forgiveness, o God,
Not justice.
For if I weighed my good deeds
Against my sin,
My sin would always weigh more.
I have nothing to stand upon,
Except the cross.

I wait for a word from God.
Your words bring hope.
Just as the third-shift worker
Looks forward to morning.
I wait for God.
I wait for God.

O sinner, put your hope in God,
For God's love for you is so great,
That He waits for you night and day.
Waiting for you to come home.
When He sees you from a distance.
He runs to meet you and welcome you
Into His Kingdom of Love.

Psalm 131 By a Theology Professor
A climbing song.

When I listen to the arguments
Calvinist, Arminian and Wesleyan
I can see some truth in all of them,
But my heart sees a God who loves me.
My soul tells me that I know almost nothing.
My eyes show me Your marvelous creation.
So as I teach theology from different schools of thought,
I remind my students that God is far beyond human understanding.
I teach them to listen to His voice
To let His Word pierce their hearts
And comfort their sorrows.

Don't trust in theology, put Your hope in God, where it belongs.

Psalm 132 Francis of Assisi
A climbing song.

Francis walked down the road,
Wondering what to do.
He'd given up the life of a soldier
And renounced being a merchant's son.
He wore the clothes of a poor peasant.
Barefoot and wearing a rough robe.
He became a beggar, begging for his food.
But what was he to do,
Now that he'd renounced his life.
That was what he wondered as
He walked down the road.

He came across an old church,
Whose walls were tumbling down.
No longer a house of God.
It was a home for rats and mice.
He heard God's voice telling him,
"Go rebuild my house."
So he went and looked it over.
Figuring out what he needed,
Started mixing mortar.
And reshaping stones.

Some men wandered by
To see what he was doing.
When he told them he was
Rebuilding this broken-down church,
They joined him in his work.
Soon they finished building the church,
And on Sunday morning,
They began to preach.

Many others came to join him.
Begging for their bread,

Doing good works for the poor,
Practicing poverty.
Clare met him in his mission
And loved God as much as he.
She created a house of sisters
Who followed the same rule.

Francis decided that to start an order,
He must get permission from the pope.
So he went to Rome
And surprised the well-dressed cardinals.

The pope wasn't too happy with this beggar.
But God gave him a dream.
The pope, a worldly man, listened to God.
And gave Francis permission to start an order.

Loving God first,
God blessed him with many followers,
And gave Francis his greatest desire,
To suffer the wounds of Christ
On his hands and feet.

There are too many stories to tell
Of Francis of Assisi.
Just remember that if you follow God.
He will give you the desires of your heart.

Psalm 133 Christian Unity
A climbing song.

It is wonderful
When Christians worship together.
It is like the Holy Spirit at Pentecost
Filling the disciples.
Who left and preached to those outside
In many different languages.

It is like the rains that pour
Upon a dried-up church.
Which, like a withered plant,
Revives, turns green and grows again.
Producing much fruit.
God hasn't forgotten us.
He pours out His blessing on His church.

Psalm 134 In God's House
A climbing song.

Praise the Lord, all you preachers,
Praise the Lord, all you singers.
Lift your hands unto God
All who sit in the church pews.
Stand up, sing and praise the Lord.

The Lord, who made heaven and earth,
Is present in this house.

Psalm 135 Praise the Lord
Praise the Lord.

Praise the name of the Lord,
Those who love the Lord.
Those who serve in His house.
Those who sing in the choir.

Praise the Lord for He is good.
He has rescued His people
From Soviet rule.
The citizens of Russia, and the Ukraine.
And all the neighboring states.
That once were under the rule
Of Communist government.
Are free at last.

They may worship God
And build themselves a church.
They may own a Bible
And listen to the Word.
They live in terrible poverty.
Barely keeping alive.
Thieves are rampant everywhere.
The mafia goes unchecked.
Life is still difficult for the people there.
The difference is
They may openly serve the Lord.

Those of us in the West
Who experience freedom of worship.
Prayed for many years.
For the Christians there.
We were very discouraged.
And could hardly believe
That the Communist rule
Would ever end.

Jimmy Carter created a war in Afghanistan.
Ronald Reagan built up star wars.
But it wasn't the American presidents
Who caused the Soviets to fall.
It was the prayer of Christians
Who brought the house down.
Though we doubted as we prayed.
Thinking that they were invincible.
God knew better than us.

Psalm 136 For God's People

Because we are free, God allows hardship to come to His people. He still loves us. He suffers with us when we go through hardship. His son's death on the cross is evidence that He suffers with us. Although God used other nations to punish Israel, He rebuked the other nations for going too far.

Thank the Lord,
For all He has done.
His love never ends.
Thank the only true God.
His love never ends.
Thank the Master of all things.
His love never ends.

He alone does great miracles.
His love never ends.
With wisdom He made the universe.
His love never ends.
He lifted the earth out of the waters.
His love never ends.
He created light with only His Word.
His love never ends.
He made the sun to give us daylight.
His love never ends.
The moon and stars guide us at night.
His love never ends.

He brought the slaves out of Egypt
His love never ends.
He freed the slaves in the United States
His love never ends.

He divided the Red Sea
His love never ends.
He saved the Union Army
His love never ends.

He defeated the rebels
His love never ends.

When the blacks lost their rights
His love never ends.
He restored civil rights.
His love never ends.
He brought Martin Luther King.
His love never ends.
When LBJ became president
His love never ends.
He got civil rights into law
His love never ends.
Through affirmative action
His love never ends.
Through the Greeks, Judah suffered.
His love never ends.
African Americans went to college.
His love never ends.
Then the Macabees brought freedom.
His love never ends.
Others became police officers.
His love never ends.
Then the Romans came.
His love never ends.
Carpenters and firemen.
His love never ends.
Herod built a new temple.
His love never ends.
Doctors and nurses.
His love never ends.

God heard the cry of his people.
His love never ends.
He ended their oppression.
His love never ends.

He will not forget them.
His love never ends.
No matter what bigotry lies in hearts.

His love never ends.
With welfare reform.
His love never ends.
Through pogroms and holocausts
His love never ends.
Some will know hardship.
His love never ends.

God still is in heaven.
His love never ends.
He will provide for the children.
His love never ends.

Give thanks to God in heaven.
His love never ends.

Psalm 137 Bitterness

When we drove home from the hospital
After our daughter had been admitted.
We thought of our sweet lovely girl –
How she wanted to be a pastor.
She had memorized much of the Bible
And she loved to learn about God.

But now she was manic and psychotic
And we didn't know what to expect.
The months dragged on,
She got better.
But she wasn't her cheery old self.
She was tired all the time.

Someone had coffee with me.
And said, "You'll get used to it.
It won't be so hard as it is now."
She was right and she was wrong.
For this wasn't her last episode.
Nor did we get used to being told
By the Christian community
That she couldn't attend
Their universities.

O God, when will it end?
The pain and the worry.
When will Christians learn
That mental illness is not a crime,
A sin, or even the fault of the parents,
But an inherited condition?

I got so angry at the university
That I couldn't be calm and forgiving.
They hurt my daughter and me
And never apologized.

It makes you want to do something
Permanent and drastic –
Like sue them for millions ... but I won't.

Psalm 138 Who is God?
By Sherye Hanson

Let me list all the good things about You, Lord.
First of all You are love.
Your love defines the word love.
We wouldn't know love
Without being loved by You.

Secondly, You are good.
When You made creation
You created it to work together,
With a grand design
And extravagant beauty.

Thirdly, You are free
So You made us to be free.
We are free to love You.
To reject You, or to respond to Your love.

Fourthly, You are more than a Creator,
The one who keeps the stars in place.
You are my Lover, Savior, and Friend.
I may be one individual in a vast universe
But I'm not forgotten by You.

This is one of those lists
That could go on forever.
When I look at the world around me,
That is usually preparing for war
Or fighting in one,
It's hard to see that You are God
And You are taking care of things.

Freedom has allowed humanity
To make some terrible mistakes.
But some day, You will come on earth.

To reign over all of us.
Until then You will look out for those
Who follow You.
You will encourage those
Who don't yet know You.
To join in Your Kingdom of love.
As long as I am living in Your will.
You will fulfill Your purpose for me.
Your love, Your goodness, Your freedom
Will last forever
And You will not forget about me.

Psalm 139 No Secrets From God
For the music director.
By Sherye Hanson

You have examined me inside and out,
I can hide nothing from You.
You know when I wake up
And when I go to sleep.
You know my thoughts, desires and actions.
My personality is not a secret to You.
You know exactly what I am about to say.

You have fenced me in on all sides.
Your hand is upon me.
I have no idea what You are doing
You are beyond me completely.

I can go to the moon and You are there.
I can go down in the deepest mine
And there You are.
I cannot escape Your presence.
Your Spirit is in my heart.
From the horizon,
To the noon day,
You are there with me,
Guiding me all the way.

I may think that the dark night hides me.
But You can see in the dark.
You can discern my deepest thoughts
As well as my spoken ones.

You created me
In my mother's uterus.
I'm in awe of the way
You put sperm and egg together.
DNA and RNA, nucleus and cell.

You know all the pieces.
Before my mother was aware
That she was pregnant,
You knew all about me.
You could see me as a fetus.
Throughout the stages of growth,
Until I was born.
You know even now how long I will live.
You have it all written down.

It is such a good feeling,
Knowing how well You know me.
There is nothing hidden from You.
I am completely under Your care.
Awake or asleep You love me.

I wish You'd rid the earth of violence and hate.
Please protect me from those
Who hurt and destroy without reason.
I want to hate them – but You love them
And died for them, too.
I pray that they will allow You
To change their hearts.

Examine me, know my heart,
Test me and know my worries.
If there is something wrong with me.
Tell me, so that I can allow Your Spirit
To change my heart.

Psalm 140 For Liberia
For the music director. By Sherye Hanson

Rescue me from the soldiers,
Who go through my village,
Shooting anyone that they can see.
They don't worry about who they hurt,
They are just on a power trip.

Protect me from the land mines,
Laid out everywhere,
They even float on the water.
Put there in the last war,
No one knows how to remove them.
Many are the men, women and children,
Who limp along on one leg.

O Lord, I cry out to You, "You are my God."
Please have mercy on my country.
Consider all the children
Who have never known peace.
Notice all the young men
Who carry guns and threaten
Their elders for bread.
They know nothing but war.
Give them a new profession.
Teach them to use their hands to plant crops
Rather than to shoot guns.

All the leaders of my country are corrupt.
They take foreign aid to build palaces for themselves.
With money from powerful countries,
They buy guns and put them in the hands of our youth.
Replace them with rulers who love You.

I know that You love the poor.
Show Your mercy on them.

Bring justice to our land.
Let peace come down like rain
And moisten the land parched from war.

Psalm 141 Drug Court

A Psalm for Bill, who went to drug court.

O Lord, I need Your help.
Today, not just tomorrow.
I'm getting out of jail.
I am relieved.
But have so much to do.
Get into treatment,
Go to court.
Get tests
Call every day.
Follow up with probation.

Keep me from temptation.
May drug dealers and users
Stay far away from me.
Keep me from that drug.

If I am disciplined by caring people
It is a kindness.
His disapproval is oil on my head.
Let me not refuse it.

I pray against those who make and sell drugs.
They are a menace to society.
I have ruined my life by using drugs.
Catch them all and put them in jail.
Let them rot there forever.

Fix my eyes on You, Ruler of my heart.
Keep me from falling away.
Protect me from the traps set for me.
Let me walk around every one
And avoid those who set them.

Keep me strong.

Psalm 142 God Hears the Mentally Ill

By Sherye Hanson. Prayer of a psychiatric patient.

I cry day and night
For mercy.
Even though He already knows.
I still cry and pray.

When I'm at my worst,
You are there walking beside me.
When there is a trap set for me
And no one else can see it but You,
I will call on You –
There is no one else who cares.

I cry to You, o God,
I say, "You are my only stability,
My only connection with reality.
Listen to me,
For my mind is confused.
I don't know if I'm being attacked
Or just paranoid.
Set me free from this prison
Of my thoughts.
Release me from the hospital
So I can go to church and
Sing praises to You.

"Then those in church
Will listen to what I have to say,
Because of Your goodness to me."

Psalm 143 For a Downsized Employee
By Sherye Hanson

God, You've gotta listen to me.
I am desperate because I lost my job.
After three months, I could use some help
From a dependable and fair God.
Don't judge me by my actions,
I'm as much of a sinner as the rest of them.

The loan company took my car yesterday,
I will soon lose my house
Because I can't pay my mortgage.
We'll be living with my parents,
And eating rice and beans.
I am so embarrassed about moving back
To living with Mom and Dad.

I remember last year, when I received a big raise.
My stock soared to the sky and we bought a new car.
Then the stock market crashed,
My company's business went south
And I was downsized.

Please don't make me wait, Lord,
I need a new job, as soon as possible.
I've been working for a fast food chain,
But my wages are barely enough for food.
My children all need clothes.
Their mother works two jobs and cannot pay the mortgage.

Teach me what Your will is
For You are my God.
May the Holy Spirit
Transform my heart.

SHERYE HANSON

I am very worried,
Help me to depend on You
For my daily bread,
The roof over our head,
And the clothing that we need.
Fill me with Your Hope.

Psalm 144 War and Peace
By Sherye Hanson

I praise the LORD, my solid ground,
Who trains my hands for war,
And my feet for battle.
He is both my loving God,
And my Desert Shield,
My base of operations
And my rearguard.
My Air Force,
And my tank patrol,
Who keeps the enemy in check.

O Lord, why do You insist on loving
Humanity with all its flaws.
Our lives pass in a nanosecond.

Come out of Your world, o Lord, come down,
Touch the volcanoes and make them smoke.
Send lighting and frighten
Send Your bombs and kill them.
Reach down, pick me up
And hold me in Your hand.
Take me out of the rising tide
Of enemies who lie with both their mouths and hands.
I will write a new song especially for You,
O God, and play it on on the keyboard.

You're the One who gives victory to armies,
Who delivers me from a stray bullet.
Pick me up and hold me,
Take me away from the lying mouths
And the hands of my enemy.

We pray that war will end forever.
So that our sons will grow to old age

And our daughters never be widows.
That none of our wealth would be wasted on war.
But our wealth would feed and house the world.

Psalm 145 A Psalm of Praise

By Sherye Hanson

I will honor You, my God the King:
Every day I will wake up in the morning
Praising Your name.

There are many people who receive honor and praise
But none of them can compare to You.
Your qualities are beyond measure.
Your love, Your power, Your presence
Are all beyond comparison.
Even Your absence, God, is too awesome to consider.
When I'm afraid I'll remember Your love.
When I'm needy I'll remember Your generosity.
When I'm overwhelmed I'll remember Your power.
During good times – I will celebrate Your love and kindness to me.

The Lord is generous and compassionate,
Slow to anger and full of love.
The Lord is good to all.
His love extends to all whom He has made.

All creation will praise You.
Those You have rescued
And made holy will honor You.
They will tell of the glory of the Kingdom of God.
Your Kingdom is an eternal kingdom.
Your dominion goes on through generation after generation.

The Lord keeps His promises.
He carries the weak
And strengthens those who are tired.
Everyone seeks You in their difficult times.
You feed them just as they need it
You are openhanded and give abundantly to all.

God's justice is tempered by mercy.
He is near whenever you call.
He says yes to those who respect Him.
He saves them when they cry.
The Lord watches over his loved ones.
He destroys the arrogant who refuse to listen.

I will sing praises to You, o God.
All creation celebrates You.

Psalm 146 Praise the Lord

I will praise the Lord,
For as long as I live.
I will praise the Lord.

I won't trust in politicians,
Generals or executives,
They cannot save.
Just like me they die,
And their plans die with them.

I will trust in God,
He has never failed me yet.
He made heaven, earth and sea,
And all the plants and animals.
The Lord is dependable.
He advocates for the oppressed,
Gives food to the hungry,
Sets prisoners free,
Gives sight to the blind,
Builds the self-esteem of those without it.
God loves the righteous.
He takes care of the alien.
The widow and her children,
He provides for.
But he stops the criminal's plans.

The Lord reigns eternal.
Our God for all generations.

Praise the Lord

Psalm 147 Sing Praises
Praise the Lord

There is nothing better that You can do,
Than to sing praises to our God.

The Lord builds up His church,
He gathers His sons and daughters
From every tongue, tribe and nation.
He heals those with broken hearts
And tends to their wounds.

He has counted the stars
And named each one.
Our God is great and powerful,
Wise beyond limits.
He cares for ordinary people,
But punishes the arrogant.

Sing thanks to God,
Make music to the Lord on the guitar.
He brings clouds and rain,
And makes the grass grow
To provide food for the cattle and the ravens.

He isn't impressed by tanks or soldiers.
He loves those who respect Him,
And trust in His Love that never ends.

Praise the Lord, of church of God,
Praise your God, people of His name.
For He protects you from the enemy
And cares for those within you.
He brings peace to those without
And brings food for your communion table.

He speaks and things happen,
Snow comes down,
Frost covers the ground,
Hail falls like pebbles,
Who can stand up to His icy blast?

He speaks again and the ice melts.
Warm breezes make the water flow.

He revealed His Word through Jesus,
To the apostles, and the epistle writers.
Once He only spoke to Israel.
But now He speaks to all through His Son.

Praise the Lord.

Psalm 148 Praise The Lord, All Creation!
Praise the Lord

Angels and heaven's army,
Praise the Lord in heaven.
Praise Him, sun, moon and stars.
Praise Him, all you universe,
Praise Him clouds and atmosphere.
Come on, creation praise His name
Because God spoke and you were made.
He set you in your eternal places
And created natural laws.

Praise the Lord on the earth.
All you species that live in the sea.
Lightning and hail, snow and clouds,
Winds all follow His orders.
Mountains and hills,
Fruit trees and conifers,
Wild and domestic animals.
Insects and birds,
Rulers and nations
Elected and inherited
Presidents and monarchs,
You men and women,
Elders and children.

Let all of you sing a chorus
Of praise to the name of the Lord.
His name is greater than all.
His beauty and power far above the rest.
O church, you are His trumpet.
O sons and daughters, you are His drum,
To tell all the nations of Him.
You are his people, close to His heart.
Praise the Lord.

Psalm 149 Praise the Lord, Church of God!
Praise the Lord.

Churches should be happy places,
Full of praise and joy.
Tired old songs should be retired.
New hymns should be written.

O, church, rejoice in Christ your head,
Jesus your brother,
The lamb of God.
Praise Him with dance, music, and shouts.
Because God delights in us.
He has taken ordinary people
And crowned them with glory and honor.
We are the sons and daughters of God.

Our praise should be a sword in the heart of sinners.
Who fear no one but the law.
Our holy life should bring conviction
To those who've lost their morality.
Our prayers should bind unjust laws, judges
And politicians from committing injustice.
Our message should be hope for the lost, oppressed and left out.
Our churches should be happy places.
Refuges for all who need refuge.

Praise the Lord.

Psalm 150 Praise Him On Instruments

Make every moment, every action, in every place
Be praise to God.
Notice all that He has done.
He created all things – including you.
He does miracles – on your behalf.
He moves mountains – that stand in your way.
Praise Him by clapping your hands.
Praise Him by shaking the tambourine.
Praise Him on strings, flute, and trumpet.
Drum bongos, clash cymbals, and rattle maracas.
Let everyone know that you love the Lord.

*